A Statement From
PRESIDENT GEORGE BUSH

"Flexible workplace policies will allow you to find and keep the best talent. And one of the most promising of these new business frontiers is telecommuting: taking advantage of new technology to enable your people to work at home one or two days a week. Clearly this exciting concept will not apply to every business or every kind of employee, but consider:

"A typical 20 minute roundtrip commute to work over the course of a year adds up to two very stressful 40 hour weeks lost on the road. But if only five percent of the commuters in L.A. County telecommuted one day each week, they'd save 205 million miles of travel each year — and keep 47,000 tons of pollutons from entering the atmosphere. So telecommuting means saving energy, improving air quality, and quality of life. Not a bad deal."

—Thursday, March 1, 1990

HAL SCHUSTER uses a computer almost 24 hours a day and is the largest home-based publisher in the world as well as a former political consultant, speechwriter, talk show host, real estate salesman, newspaper columnist and junior accountant. His writing has ranged from comic books to a chapter in a popular college textbook. He is the author of *The Films of Elvis* and *Drug Wars*, and is currently writing both *Operation Exodus* and *Caution: Computer at Work*.

PAUL and SARAH EDWARDS are work-at-home seminar leaders and speakers. The Edwards regularly lecture at the University of California, Los Angeles and at the University of Southern California, contribute a regular column to *Home Office Computing Magazine* and serve as hosts for the Working at Home Forum on Compuserve, an information network with 750,000 subscribers as well as the Home Office Radio Show on National Business Radio and the Wake Up For Success radio show in Los Angeles. Their bestselling *Working From Home* was the first major book in the field.

VALERIE HOOD runs a very successful word processing and desktop publishing business in Los Angeles and teaches a regular course, "Starting a Part Time/Full Time Word Processing Business" for The Learning Annex.

IRVIN FELDMAN, a Certified Management Accountant, has run his own private practice specializing in small business accounting since 1980 as well as taught accounting for eight years at Pace University, Jersey State College, Nassau Community College and York College of the City University of New York and written for *The Journal of Accounting, Auditing and Finance* and *Management Accounting*.

STEVEN EDWARDS, an 11 year veteran of using computers for marketing and sales, has written extensively for *Home Office Computing*, Hewett Packard and other computer companies.

JULIE ANN JOHNSON has written for *Teleconnect* and *Telephony Magazine*, as well as *The Telecommunication Managers Plain-english Guide*, *A Guide To Vending* and a number of short reports on mail order and telemarketing for the small and home business. Julie also runs a successful home-based company selling business and vending opportunities nationwide by mail.

DALE LEWALLEN is a product analyst and trends watcher for *PC Week* magazine

MIKE MYERS develops and creates presentations for his consulting business.

HOW TO USE A COMPUTER IN YOUR HOME OFFICE

By Hal Schuster

With Paul and Sarah Edwards

electronic cottage   las vegas, nv

For additional or bulk copies for
your club, business, school or
organization please contact:
Pioneer Books, Inc.
5715 N. Balsam Rd.
Las Vegas, NV 89130

Library of Congress Cataloging-in-Publication Data
Hal Schuster, 1955—
  How to Use a Computer in Your Home Office

  1.   How to Use a Computer in Your Home Office (business)
 I. Title

Published by Electronic Cottage, an imprint of Pioneer Books,
Inc., 5715 N. Balsam Rd., Las Vegas, NV, 89130.

First Printing, 1990

The 101 best full-time and part-time businesses to start with your computer for 1990

1. Analyzing Research Data, Polls & Surveys
2. Auditing Services
3. Babysitting Referral Service
4. Beta Testing Software
5. Billing & Invoicing Service
6. Bookkeeping & Accounting services
7. Business Broker
8. Catalog Publisher
9. Checking Employment Applications
10. Collection/Skip Tracing Agency
11. Computer Bulletin Board Services
12. Computer Consulting
13. Computer Graphics/Presentations
14. Computer Programming
15. Computer Tutoring
16. Computer Novelties & Gifts
17. Contest Organizer
18. Copywriter
19. Customizing Commercial Software
20. Custom Programming
21. Data Converting Service
22. Data Entry Overload for companies
23. Data Processing Service
24. Debugging Software
25. Deposition Digesting
26. Desktop Publishing Services
27. Desktop Video
28. Directory Publishing

66. Medical Transcription Service
67. Music - Teaching, Composing
68. Newsletter Publishing
69. Nursing Registry for Patients
70. Office Automation Consultant
71. Out-of-Town Business Service
72. Payroll Preparation
73. Private Investigator
74. Publicist, Public Relations
75. Public Opinion Surveys
76. Referral Service
77. Reminder Service
78. Renting Computer Time
79. Repairing Computers
80 Research Service
81. Resume and Portfolio Preparation, Writing
82. Reunion Planning
83. Roommate Finding & Matching Service
84. Scholarship Research Service
85. Second Medical Opinion Referral Service
86. Seminar Organizer, Promoter
87. Show Promoter for Consumers or Trade
88. Sign-Making Service
89. Software Writer
90. Software Location Service
91. Sports League Statistics
92. Tax Preparation & Consulting
93. Trade Association Operation
94. Training Agent; Broker; Vendor
95. Transcribing Court Reporter Notes
96. Transcribing Radio and TV Programs
97. Translation Service
98. Typesetting Service
99. Used Computer Broker
100. Word Processing Service
101. Writer—Technical, Trade, Documentation

CONTENTS

CONTENTS

CONTENTS

Dedicated to my father, Irwin, of blessed memory. Without him there would be no book. He taught me the world is full of opportunities and life is a grand adventure.

INTRODUCTION

Several centuries ago almost everyone ran a home business. They either farmed or owned a small shop where they made things, provided services or sold what people needed. England was known as a nation of shopkeepers; America was no different.

Families lived and worked together. Of necessity fathers were close to sons, husbands to wives. They spent their lives together.

Then came the dawn of the industrial revolution. Massive machinery began to produce standardized goods on assembly lines. It took large amounts of capital to purchase the necessary heavy machinery. Cities blackened by smokestacks replaced small towns and families were ripped asunder. New social problems became rampant.

Now events have changed life once again. New lifestyles made possible by the development of microelectronics, including copiers, computers, FAX and much more lead to a better present and an even more promising future. The massive edge held by large corporations with incredible investments in capital goods has disappeared. A smart small business owner can now successfully compete using the latest technology in their own homes or small offices. The machineries of which corporate America was so proud lie rusting while the dinosaur corporations devour each other and slowly die.

The number of self-employed is now growing 3 to 4 times faster than salaried workers.

During the recession of '81 and '82, large corporations cut 1.7 million employees while small businesses added 2.3 million.

In 1985, industries dominated by small businesses grew by over 5% while those dominated by large companies shrank by almost one percent.

David Birch has found that four out of five new jobs are created by companies with less than 20 employees.

The most interesting thing about the stock market plunge of that dark Monday a few years ago is how little impact it had. A lesser plunge in 1929 threw the entire country into depression. The recent event answered the unasked question: what if they gave a stock market crash and nobody came? The stock market no longer represents the business of America.

Because data gathers slowly, all of these numbers are prior to the recent rash of merger and acquisition activity. This further shrank many major corporations and eliminated several altogether. The trends in favor of small businesses grew stronger.

In '85, companies with over 500 employees generated 39% of GNP while 35% was produced by smaller companies (15% was government and 3.5% agriculture). This relationship has undoubtedly reversed itself since. Corporate America is now smaller than small business America.

The handwriting is on the wall. Small businesses, including home businesses, are the engine that drives our economy. They create the new jobs and the breakthrough fields.

The growth of small and home-based businesses solves many of the nation's worst problems. Families are reunited. Pollution from automobiles is reduced. Rush hour traffic shrinks.

Whether it's a Steve Jobs tinkering in his garage and creating the Apple computer or someone whose name most people will never know carving out a wonderful life of productivity and family, the home office is the place to watch!

SECTION 1

THE ELECTRONIC COTTAGE REVOLUTION IN YOUR HOME

CHAPTER 1

A NEW DAWN

A new workday is dawning in America. A workday that begins with a leisurely walk down the hall from the kitchen to a spare bedroom or den. There is no fighting traffic, no daily commute . . . no rousting the children from their beds before the sun comes up to drag them off to daycare. The office of today, for those who choose it, can just as well be in an urban townhouse or apartment building, a single-family home or rural cottage as in the familiar downtown or suburban office building.

In observance of it's centennial, *The Wall Street Journal* commissioned the Roper Organization to conduct The American Way of Buying Survey and discovered that ten percent of all work done in the United States today is already being performed in people's homes. The people who are working from home are people like you and like us. They range from programmers who are writing the software you see in today's computer magazines and computer stores to caterers and consultants, contractors and craftspeople, all of whom are earning a living full or part time from labor they do in their homes. You might be surprised to know that even an international bank with branches in Europe is headquartered in a home in Colorado Springs.

So if you are thinking you too would enjoy the freedom and the convenience of being your own boss in a home-based business, you are not alone. Nor will you be considered an oddity. According to Link Resources' newest research, over 26 million people work at home some portion of the week and over five million people began doing job-related work at home during the past 12 months. Twelve hundred new home businesses begin every day — that is one every 71 seconds. That means a new home business has begun somewhere since you began reading this book.

Small business, of which home business is a significant part, is big business today. It's the engine that is driving the American economy, providing half the nation's workers and two out of every three first jobs. Pacific Bell says 52% of their Yellow Page ads are from small businesses. While the daily headlines continue to tell us about big businesses cutting back, the engine of small business continues to grow. In this introduction, we will tell you why such growing numbers of people are striking out on their own from home and why. If you have a dream, now is a good time for you to join them.

We have been described as pioneers because we began working from home in the 1970's. At that time working at home was unusual for white collar workers in the prime of their careers. In fact, our neighbors believed Paul was unemployed.

As much as we'd like to accept titles as pioneers, we discovered in researching our book *Working From Home*, that many homeworkers had preceded us. In fact, the original home offices belonged to the ancient Romans. The room where the head of the household managed his money and accounts was called a tablinum.

In the Middle Ages, European merchants' shops and artisans' work areas were located on the main floor of their homes. The family living was done in a single shared room upstairs.

The combination of work and home migrated to America. Paul Revere did his silversmithing in the front of his home in Boston that you can see on the Freedom Trail today. Some of you may even have had parents or grandparents who operated mom and pop businesses, living either upstairs or in the back of their businesses. Of course, our President continues to this day to work at home.

The Industrial Revolution, however, pulled people from their homes and farms to staff factories and offices. The automobile enabled the physical separation of home and work by many miles, leading to the development of bedroom suburbs and the familiar daily commute that today collectively occupies millions of hours of time while the automobiles we sit in pollute our air.

History has a way of repeating itself, so by 1980 when we began writing *Working From Home*, rather than considering us oddities, we found people were curious about how they too might work from home. In fact, we began writing *Working From Home* because so many people were asking us, "How do you do that? That's what I want to do." We knew a book was needed.

Once *Working from Home* was published in 1985, however, we often were told that this was nothing more than a passing fad. In his book *Megatrends*, John Naisbitt said it would never catch on. Now Naisbitt himself works from home in Telluride, Colorado and our book is in its third edition.

Why are so many people beginning to work from home? Fundamentally, there are two reasons. First, because people want to. Second, because recent changes in the economy and electronic technology make it possible.

CHAPTER 2

WHY PEOPLE WANT
TO WORK FROM HOME

Our society has changed from an industrial to an information and service economy. This transformation has brought disruptions. In the 1980's over ten million factory workers lost their jobs. Only three out of five of them found other work. Managers and professionals seeking to climb the corporate pyramid found mid-level positions were disappearing as the corporate hierarchy began looking less like a pyramid and more like a pancake.

As disheartening as these shifts are, information-age technology also creates opportunities. Computers and high-speed communication make it possible for anyone to start a business at home and for most jobs to be worked at home. After the October, 1989 San Francisco earthquake forced many people to work at home because of damage to the freeway system, many of these people refused to return to offices. They liked working at home. More and more people today want to be their own boss. Repeatedly as we travel across the country, we hear people saying things like: "I've been told 'It's none of your business,' so often that I've decided to start my own business." Or "I want to set my own hours and keep what I earn for myself. I'm tired of the rat race. I'm fed up with nine to five."

Does this sound familiar? Of course, we know that succeeding in a home-based business of your own usually takes more than eight hours of work a day, but whatever success you have belongs to you.

There are also financial reasons for wanting to work from home. It's a legitimate way to keep more of the money you earn from the tax collector. After Tax Reform, having one's own business is now one of the few tax shelters available to the middle class. That means you have a chance to be one of the five people in a hundred people in this country who, according to the Social Security Administration, are financially independent at age 65.

A recent survey reported in *USA TODAY* showed that the love of one's family is the value

Americans cherish most. And working from home makes it easier for us to be with family and loved ones.

When we were in our last year of college, we looked with mixed feelings at the future because it appeared that 40 years would need to pass and we would have to retire before we could once again have much time together. But working from home and working together has made it possible to open new dimensions in our relationship and enjoy each other's company while we're still in the prime of our careers.

So, you see, working from home meets very real, practical needs. Here are several snapshots of real people who like yourself began to view working from home as a solution to creating a healthier, wealthier and happier life.

Working from home means less stress

For many people like forty-seven-year-old Marilyn Miller, working from home takes the stress out of her otherwise hectic daily routine. Marilyn was a working mother, employed as a college professor when she developed a life-threatening, stress-related illness. Doctors told her she would have to change her lifestyle. She opened a private practice from her Malibu, California home as a career counselor, helping others find career alternatives. She tells us she saves a minimum of an hour a day commuting in congested traffic.

Working from home makes balancing family and career easier

Working from home is an appealing option for the increasing number of two-career couples and single parents. Judy Wunderlich of Schaumburg, Illinois is a good example. Because she had two small children, Judy decided to quit her job and start a home-based typesetting service. However, typesetting for others often still required her to work on-site, so she started a temporary employment agency placing typesetters, graphic designers, keyliners and desktop publishers with Chicago companies. Working only 20 hours a week in her first year of business, she earned $54,000.

Judy says "My biggest achievement is running a business without having to put my two children (who are both under three years old) in day care. I designed my office so I can watch my kids all the time. My biggest mistake was not doing this earlier. I made back the money I spent on equipment in just three weeks."

It's not just women who are finding working from home makes parenting easier. Wayne Dunlap is a single father. He finds running his business, Education Network from his home in Indianapolis, Indiana, makes being a single parent of teen age children a lot easier. Dunlap earns a comfortable living as a sales trainer, teaching people in the computer industry how to sell goods and services.

Working from home provides security against layoffs and mergers

When David Eliason was laid off from his job as a news director for a Dubuque, Iowa radio station, he turned his hobby into a business. His business is called Professional Audio and he designs and installs sound systems for churches, auditoriums, racetracks, office buildings and theaters. He also operates Mobile Music Machine, a mobile disk jockey service. He has one full-time and ten part-time employees and grosses $200,000. He says, "The turning point for me was getting fired."

Millions of Americans face similar prospects as companies downsize. From 1980 to 1987, Fortune 500 companies shrunk by over three million people. Change is not limited to the largest corporations. Privately-held mid-sized companies are changing hands in record numbers. So it's not surprising that Robert Half International found that the #1 fear of executives in America is the fear of losing their job because of mergers or acquisitions.

At age 35, Karen Rubin of Los Angeles had held more than 150 jobs, but says she has never been fired other than when companies reorganized, were merged or acquired. After she was let go from a cable network, she decided that starting her own business couldn't possibly be any less secure than her job history. Since she had always been a trouble shooter on her jobs, she launched a company called Organizer Extraordinaire. She helps individuals and organizations get organized. Karen says, "The greatest influence on me has been all the negative jobs I've had. I wanted to create an experience for myself and others that was totally the opposite. When I leave a job now, people give me a hug and kiss."

Working from home means a way out of dead-end jobs into more meaningful work

When David Chazin became burned out on his job in advertising and marketing, he read an article about laser cartridges and had the idea to start his own business, LaserTeck, remanufacturing laser and printer cartridges. Now he says "It used to be that when the alarm rang in the morning I wasn't enthused. I don't use an alarm anymore. When I wake up in the morning, I can't wait to get started."

Working from home let's you be your own boss

Ray Jassin worked in law libraries for many years but like more than half of all Americans, he always wanted the satisfaction of being his own boss. After seven years in business, Ray earns over a half million dollars a year running his own law library management service in Huntington, New York.

The number of people deciding to be their own bosses is growing at the rate of one and a third million new small businesses each year. It's estimated that at least a third of these begin in people's homes. Some of these will grow as others have before them into Amways, Apple Computers, Baskin-Robbins', Domino's Pizzas, Hershey Foods', Hallmark Cards', Hewlett-Packard's, Mrs. Fields Cookies', Nike Shoes', Playboy, Readers Digest, and Walt Disney.

While the number of small business failures used to deter people from venturing out on their own, those statistics are improving too. It used to be that four out of five small businesses were gone within five years. The most recent statistic from the Small Business Administration is this number is down to three out of five. We're nearing the point where what has been called a failure rate should be called a success rate. We anticipate that as more people learn how to succeed in their own business, the number of successes will continue to grow.

CHAPTER 3

TECHNOLOGY MAKES IT POSSIBLE

One reason that a growing number of people are succeeding in their own businesses is because today's service and information businesses require little start-up capital and can be conducted as easily from home as anywhere. Technology, which is getting smaller, cheaper and more capable, makes it possible to work from home as productively as anywhere.

When we began working from home, other than the standard desk, chair and filing cabinet, we had only two pieces of electronic equipment to help us function effectively: a Selectric typewriter and an answering machine. Unfortunately more than half of our callers hung up as soon as the recorded message began. Then computers and copy machines wouldn't fit in average-sized closets.

Today we have a laptop and two desktop computers, a copy machine the size of a brief case, a fax, four modems, a cellular phone and a laser and an ink jet printer, not to mention two answering machines that rarely elicit hang-ups. At the time we interviewed the seven people we've introduced to you, their combined home offices were equipped with 14 computers, 13 printers, 7 modems, 7 answering machines, 3 copiers, 2 faxes, 2 cellular phones, and one dedicated typesetting system.

Why so much equipment? Because technology enables businesses to operate from home and it helps solve the major problem people experience in working from home. We find that being taken seriously as a bona fide business by customers and suppliers is the #1 problem of operating a home-based business.

As Joe Gadoury, who with his wife Deborah, operates a New Jersey animation and special effects firm told us, "Some corporations above a certain size need to see chrome and glass." A lack of an office or store front sometimes results in lost contracts, less attention from suppliers, and most banks will not grant merchant status to home-based businesses so they can be paid with Mastercard and Visa.

We believe that the right technology provides many solutions to this problem. If you are good at what you do, a personal computer, a laser printer, desktop publishing software, a modem, a fax, perhaps a toll-free "800" number together with some street smarts can solve most credibility problems.

Manufacturers of office equipment, furniture and supplies are taking an interest in the home-based business. Equipment is being scaled down to meet the space limitations of home offices. We'll see more of this in the future as single-function equipment becomes integrated. Arno Penzias, 1978 Nobel winner in physics and a vice president of Bell Labs predicts that the personal computer of the future will merge printers, scanners, copiers, fax machines, modems, telephones, video conferencing systems and filing cabinets into one package.

Software and technology can save time and make tedious tasks less time consuming. Service and support from the growing number of retailers interested in the home/office market make handling purchasing decisions and setting up and maintaining an office less burdensome. So as you can see, the future of becoming your own boss from your spare bedroom, basement or garage is bright. Perhaps you will be like thousands we talk with who begin by bringing work home from their job and then ask themselves, "Why not start a part-time business on the side?" We find those part-time home businesses often progress to become full-time businesses. Almost every day on the Working From Home forum on CompuServe, which we began in 1983, we hear from people whose part-time business begins to require so much more time and produces so much more income that they leave their jobs to work full-time in their own business. They tell us they're so much more excited about their sideline business than going off to their job the next morning that the transition is a welcome one.

We've also noticed that once the full-time business begins to grow, one person working from home often becomes two. Spouses begin helping with the business part-time and then, if the business continues to prosper, they join in full-time as well.

This progression is part of the human drive to achieve greater and greater control over our lives. We're seeing this drive for freedom sweep across the world right now. As long as we yearn to be the captains of our own ships, there will always be the drive to venture out on our own. Now the economy not only allows, but supports and in some cases demands that we take the leap to steer our own economic futures. The trend toward corporate downsizing and even downturns in the economy feed those flames.

We began by saying that a new workday is dawning in America — one in which the office can be at home as well as anywhere your heart desires. It's happening because it makes sense — dollars and sense to individuals and families who are more productive because they are happier, healthier and wealthier. And to communities who will benefit from cleaner air and less congestion.

It's becoming the New American Dream and as you think about your personal dream, just keep in mind one thing, someone's going to do it. It might as well be you.

CHAPTER 4

PICKING A FUTURE

If you're looking for a way you can make money with a personal computer, you are in the right place at the right time. Today is a time of opportunity. Corporations are consolidating, decentralizing and downsizing. New technologies are creating new needs for services and skills. It's one of those rare times that comes along once in a lifetime, if at all.

Several years ago we appeared on a Denver radio station. In the lobby of the station was a blow-up of a 1925 newspaper article with a photograph of a small white frame house. Dominating the house was a radio tower attached to the roof. The house was the home of the founders of the station. A doctor and his wife had started the radio station in their living room. The doctor played the violin and his wife sang. With the help of their friends and their infant son, who played the spoons, they entertained a growing listening audience. Today that radio station is the largest one in Denver.

Now, can you imagine starting a radio station today in your home? It is possible to start a computer-related business in your living room and have it grow into a large business of tomorrow. Personal computers are now about where radio was at that time.

A window of opportunity is open. The introduction of the automobile, radio and television opened windows of opportunity in the past. Most of us were too young to take advantage of those. Yet the opportunities created by the popularization of the personal computer today will be as far reaching, and perhaps more so, than those of the past.

The personal computer offers almost unlimited possibilities for profitable businesses. If you are already in the computer field, you will find that you are uniquely qualified to start many of these businesses. Even if you are a computer novice, or don't own a computer yet, you will still find, perhaps to your surprise, that there are many computer-related businesses well-suited to you.

People have already begun making money with personal computers. Every year, half a million new businesses file tax returns. That's a new business every 63 seconds. More of these each year are computer-related. We'll introduce you to some of these new businesses and the people who are starting them. You'll meet people of all ages and widely differing backgrounds. People like yourself, who had an idea or a dream, and went ahead to live it.

You'll find these successful entrepreneurs have started a business with their computer for the same reasons that undoubtedly interest you. They want to supplement their income, find a more rewarding and challenging career, create a tax shelter and find a way for their computer to pay for itself.

So whether you're thinking of a sideline business to supplement your salary or a full-time business, now is the time to take advantage of the opportunities.

Someone is going to profit from the new possibilities computers are opening to us. It might as well be you!

CHAPTER 5

THE MANY BUSINESS POSSIBILITIES

In starting a business, you can choose one with a proven demand such as word processing or you can be a pioneer and do something new.

Having led seminars for thousands of people starting businesses with their computers, we would like to introduce a sampling of the businesses you can start. Since the possibilities are many, the question is where to begin. Let's look at a number of money-making opportunities.

Computers help people work with words, numbers and symbols.

Using word processing and desktop publishing, you can use your computer in a variety of ways. You can start a word processing service typing letters and documents. You can manage mailing lists, and/or prepare term papers, dissertations or screenplays. You can provide cataloging and indexing services or edit newsletters. You can even offer typesetting.

With database management programs, you can use your computer to start a business that provides filing, mailing list and record keeping services that help people manage customer and client lists, inventories or personnel records.

Project management software will allow you to do scheduling, planning, resource allocation, "perting" and critical paths.

With electronic spreadsheet, bookkeeping and accounting programs, you can start a bookkeeping service or use a computer to provide financial services. These can include stock market analysis, budgeting projections, investment planning, record keeping, cash flow and financial planning.

With communications programs, you can communicate with other computers nearby or afar and start a business providing research services. You can also make referral and reservation services to help people find a restaurant, an apartment, a room mate, a babysitter or a lost pet.

You can create graphics with a computer which means you can create computer art, design clothing, create slide shows and plot test scores or financial information.

The computers create needs as well as provide opportunities. These needs provide further opportunities. Individuals and organizations need someone to repair computers and teach people to use computers and select computer systems.

Opportunities now exist to sell or rent new or used computers or to write or design software.

You can create computer accessories and aids to help in using computers or design furniture for computers or other office electronics.

There is a new demand for newsletters or magazine articles about computers.

You can even counsel people about their fears of computers.

Turning your talents and skills into a business

If you are not interested in the world of computers itself, chances are you can still use a computer to turn your interests or hobbies into a profitable business. You can use a computer to enhance the productivity and performance of whatever business interests you have, giving your business a competitive edge. People are now using computers effectively in sales, career planning, nutrition counseling and astrological charting. They use computers to make job referrals, compose and teaching music, and write books, magazines and newsletters. They perform travel planning, party planning and catering. They teach and provide security services. The list of opportunities almost seems endless.

The best opportunities haven't been thought of yet

Because computers help us solve problems, the last and most exciting area of opportunity is the many businesses that haven't been thought of yet. For example, in Nashville, a 13 year old boy, noticing that people were complaining about their orders being filled in a McDonald's store, went home and developed a program for cueing orders. He then went on to sell the program and the computers that ran it to all the McDonald's stores in that area.

A woman in San Francisco, noticing that personal computers and word processing pools were replacing the personal secretaries of the past, decided to form an executive reminder service using her computer's capabilities. This grew to become a popular gift buying service for busy executives.

An auto mechanic who attended one of our seminars developed a business locating auto parts for different wrecking yards and providing the information via computer to interested customers.

The possibilities are limited only by your imagination. You can choose to be a pioneer. Less than ten years ago the popular personal computer businesses were ideas in the minds of people who perceived needs they could fill.

They decided to innovate and although that meant risk, they took the chance. Experimenting and failing along the way, they proved what Adele Scheele, author of *Skills for Success*, has found: successful people have more failures than unsuccessful ones. The reason — successful people experiment more.

CHAPTER 6

FIVE POPULAR BUSINESSES

As you think about choosing a computer related business, you can pioneer a new idea or select a proven business concept. Let's look at five proven and popular business choices. Because of today's rapidly growing market, these businesses can be started easily and can turn a profit relatively quickly if done properly. The first three are businesses you can start with or without a background in computers. The last two are businesses best suited to those already in the computer field

Word processing services

In this popular business, you use your computer like a fancy typewriter, doing everything a typing service would do only faster and better.

Barbara Elman started Ace Computer Script in 1978 and introduced word processing services to scriptwriters. She says this is a good time to go into word processing because people have come to recognize its value. Since word processing is becoming so popular, however, you may have some competition, so Barbara suggests specializing in a particular market. She chose scriptwriting because she was a writer herself. Other markets needing word processing include law firms, large businesses seeking overload services, very small businesses and college students and faculty.

Electronic bookkeeping services

Electronic bookkeeping is another rapidly growing business. It provides all the services of a regular bookkeeper such as keeping accounts receivable and accounts payable and preparing tax reports and financial statements. It also provides related services such as billing and inventory control.

Tom and Nancy Nickle decided to start a bookkeeping service to pay for the IBM PC they wanted to buy. They began approaching medical, dental and real estate offices when they stumbled onto a unique niche — freight billing. They provide billing, auditing and reporting services to freight departments of large companies. They advise people interested in starting an electronic bookkeeping service to be imaginative and come up with as many ideas as possible for who can use these services. Then experiment by approaching different markets until you find your particular niche.

Information research services

With an information research service, you use your computer to search for information your clients need and otherwise find in such places as libraries, trade associations, government archives and newspapers. Instead you search computerized databases that have organized this information for rapid search and retrieval by computer.

Clients pay you to research everything from the market for Christmas trees in Hawaii to current trends in the Venezuelan construction industry. Electronic research can save your customers hours in the library or over the phone tracking down information. One minute of "online" computer research is equivalent to two hours in the library.

Researcher Sue Rugge was among the first to offer a computerized information service. The company she started, Information on Demand, is now known throughout the country. Sue finds that although people are beginning to recognize the value of a computer research service, it is still new to think of information as a commodity. She feels that marketing is the key to success in this business.

Writing computer software

The largest area of growth in the computer field today is in software development. Although there are over 50,000 pieces of personal computer software on the market, many applications remain to be written. Programmers of all ages and interests are writing software programs for both fun and profit. Even people with no programming experience are having ideas for software and teaming up with programmers to create it.

Psychologist Elizabeth Scott and Lucy Ewell, a computer systems analyst, began writing software games for girls. They had noticed that software manufacturers were not writing games that appealed to girls and decided to fill the niche provided by this huge market.

The key is to identify something that someone needs done and develop a program for doing it easier, better or quicker. Norm Goode, former Publisher of MicroMoonlighter Newsletter, recommends that aspiring software writers focus on a major market for software — education, entertainment or specialized vertical business markets for which little software is available.

Computer consulting

The sudden explosion of the personal computer into our lives has left most of the business and professional world eager to get on board, yet many lack the knowledge to do so. Churches, sports organizations, lawyers, doctors, even beauty salons all want to use computers in their work. The result is a growing demand for the computer consultant, someone with the necessary expertise to help select, set up and train others in the use of computer hardware and software. Since only half of American businesses have computerized, consulting services will continue to be in demand for some time to come.

Bill Slavin started a computer consulting firm specializing in helping managers use personal computers for such activities as long range planning and project management. He believes personal computers open many opportunities for consulting, but if you intend to consult in this field you have to specialize and be an expert at what you do. "In the computer field, it's like speaking French, you can't fake it. You have to be the best and let people know that you're the best."

CHAPTER 7

CHOOSING
THE RIGHT BUSINESS

We've mentioned only a sampling of the many opportunities that are available for starting a business with a personal computer.

Finding a business that's right for you, your particular niche, is more than knowing what can be done or what others are doing. It's using your imagination to combine the capabilities of a computer with your unique interests and skills to provide what people are willing to pay for.

We agree with Norm Goode, "Don't be tempted to fall into the trap of some 'canned' business scheme you read about in a national advertisement." Norm has found that "for a while the personal computer industry was almost free from scams, but now that computers have become the new buzzword, there are shady types out there seeking to get some fast cash." You will do better using your own creativity to find a niche you are uniquely qualified to fill.

Michael Anderson once traveled across the country for a major company selling limited partnerships in oil and gas. Then he realized computers could solve the problems traveling sales professionals have lugging their materials from place to place. He turned this idea into Broadmoor Computer Systems, providing computer hardware and software to meet this need. He suggests that people wanting to start a computer-related business take whatever experience they've had and build on that. "Just keep building on what you learn. It's the greatest pyramid scheme in the world."

There are many ways to find your own magic formula.

Finding your niche

Discovering the business that is best for you involves identifying what you are most suited for and most interested in doing. You can use your current position and previous work experience as a springboard, draw on talents you may have overlooked or turn your hobbies and outside interests into a business. The key is to select something you really enjoy doing.

Using your current position and previous experience

If you like the work you are doing now, start where you are. For example, if you're working in a jewelry store and you like this line of work, ask yourself how you could take your knowledge of jewelry, or of retailing and merchandising, and use that knowledge and skill to create a computer-related business. You could start with your employer and assist him or her in selecting a computer system for keeping track of merchandise, managing mailing lists and following commodity prices. From this experience you could then begin consulting with other jewelers explaining how they could use computers in their business.

It's the process of combining knowledge from your special skill or discipline with the capabilities of the computer that makes the most successful business opportunities. Ask yourself, "Using a computer, how could I provide a solution to a problem in my field and turn that into my own business? What can I add from my prior experience that could enhance this new business?

We know of an instant printer, for example, whose background was in engineering. He was able to use what he knew about computers as an engineer to custom design software for running his instant print shop. It worked for his business so he began selling his programs to other printers.

If you would prefer getting out of what you're doing now and doing something different, inventory your talents and skills. Ask yourself, "What do I really want to do? Can I use what I'm most interested in as a door to something new?"

Pursuing a hobby or personal interest

Daniel Montague was an insect exterminator, but computers were his hobby. Today he operates Micro-Instructional. The company produces a line of audio cassette tapes that teach listeners how to use most popular models of personal computers.

Gil Gordon was a personnel director for a large pharmaceutical company. He also possessed a fascination for the growing trend of telecommuting. Today he is Gil Gordon Associates, consulting with companies interested in setting up programs for telecommuting or other alternative work site projects.

Barbara Elman, who we mentioned earlier, had been typing for some time, although what she actually wanted to do was write. She didn't know much about computers, but she could see the possibilities they offered for writers. She pioneered this exciting application. Since starting, she's gotten into desktop publishing and has moved on into the movie industry.

Recognizing your hidden talents

Often the best business idea is right under your nose but you don't think of it because it is a natural part of what you do every day.

What do people say you do well? Interview your friends. Think about the things you've heard people say. They will often note, "You know, you really ought to start a such and such," or "You really ought to do so and so. You're so good at that."

Choosing something you enjoy

Whatever you decide to do, choose something you really enjoy doing. Starting a business takes time and energy and when you like what you're doing, it's a lot easier to get yourself to do all the work involved. As freelance programmer Jim Milburn says, "When you get into something you like doing, you won't have to fight yourself doing it."

The people we've introduced you to all chose businesses where they could do what they really love to do. It's easy, however, to get swept away with a popular moneymaking idea only to discover that you don't like doing it.

A woman in one of our seminars almost fell into this trap.

She had been doing bookkeeping for several years and came to the seminar to learn how she could start an electronic bookkeeping service. After listening to us discuss selecting a business, she remembered how much she enjoyed teaching when she was younger. She decided to explore starting a business teaching children how to use computers.

To discover what appeals most to you think about what you do on your day off, and on vacation. Examine what you would leap out of bed for. What magazines, newsletters and books do you read? What headlines catch your eye?

Remember when you were a child? What did you love doing?

What have you always said, "Someday I'm going to...."

Imagine it's the last day of your life. As you look back on your life, how would you fill out this statement, "I sure wish I had ...."

Knowing what people need

Successful businesses fill a need. Once you have identified your skills, talents and interests, think about what people need. What are they willing to pay for? Look at the trends of the day — changes in population...new technologies...more women with careers...more people working at home ... single parents ... robotics eliminating many jobs.

What do these trends suggest about what people need? What problems do you see people having? Listen for what people complain about. What people complain about finding, for example, can be the basis for a referral or location service for everything from baby-sitters to software programs.

What do people hate doing? Most people don't like fixing, cleaning, researching or performing detail work. That's one reason book-keeping services prosper.

What holes do you notice in the market, a need that no one's filling? Before the Apple computer, microcomputers were the domain of the hobbyist and the hacker. Steven Jobs recognized a much wider market awaited a computer that was "user friendly." Adam Osborne responded to a hole in the market for a portable computer complete with software for under $2,000.

To help anticipate what people will be needing, you can read books such as *Megatrends 2000*.

CHAPTER 8

WHAT MAKES A BUSINESS SUCCESSFUL

Nationally two businesses out of five are still in business after five years. This is better than it sounds, because nine of ten business closures are voluntary, either because of retirement or the owners deciding to shift to a more profitable or personally rewarding field.

Many businesses fail. Reportedly, the two principle reasons for business failure are, first, a lack of capital and proper money management and, second, a lack of experience, know-how and information.

The characteristics of a successful business

A classic study of new businesses found that after a three-year period nearly twice the percentages of female-owned and managed businesses were successful as male-owned and managed businesses! Here's what the study showed to be the characteristics of successful businesses:

1. Their owners had taken 6 to 10 months to research and prepare for their businesses.

2. They used professional advisers and consultants in setting up their business.

3. They had taken business-related courses and read regularly about business management. They had done their homework.

4. They started their business with more modest expectations for success than the unsuccessful entrepreneurs.

What you need to know

Results such as these show that to succeed in business, it's what you know that counts. You'll need to know your stuff. Be on top of the market, manage your money effectively, know your own strengths and weaknesses, master your computer and where to get the help you need.

Knowing your stuff

You'll need to be an expert in your particular field and your business. Fortunately, because we live in an information age, you can become an expert in your business and your field without years of study or a long apprenticeship. Here's some ideas for how you can quickly gain the expertise you'll need:

1. Join professional organizations and trade associations. Become active in the local chapters. To locate the associations and organizations in your particular field, you can check *Gale's Encyclopedia of Associations*. It is available in public libraries or on-line through gateway services such as Compuserve's IQuest service or Dialog Information Services.

2. Read trade and professional journals and special interest magazines and newsletters. *Gale's Encyclopedia of Associations* tells you which associations and organizations have their own newsletter or journal.

3. Attend trade shows and exhibits, go to workshops and seminars, read books, listen to tapes by leading authorities in your field.

4. Take a temporary job or volunteer to work in a related business.

If you do this ground work, you will know 95% of what's known in a field and 98% more than others in the field.

Knowing your market

You will need to know specifically who needs the services or products you have to offer. Do your research. Talk to prospective customers and clients. Learn everything you can about them, their needs and interests. Do they already know they need your product or service?

Do they have the money and willingness to pay for what you have to offer? Are they already using a similar product or service?

Scout out the competition. Buy their products. Get their brochures and price lists. You can find your competition by looking in the yellow pages or by talking to the Chamber of Commerce.

Interview them. Survey your competitions' customers to find out what they like and don't like. Find out how what you will offer will differ in quality, price, variety and level of service from your competition.

Knowing your money

Because the nature of our economy is changing from an industrial base to an information and service base, many of the rules about money and money management are changing. As a general rule, it used to take a lot of capital to start a business. Today, it's possible to open a business with minimal start-up capital. Other than the expense of their computer, people have started businesses for as little as $50 to $100.

Lack of capital or mismanagement of money is still a primary reason businesses fail. It is important to know your money situation, but don't let lack of money intimidate you. Figure out now what the real money needs are for your new business. If the amount you need will require borrowing, try to learn how to do what you need to do without burdening your new venture with debt.

Don't spend much money until you know you have a marketable business. We know of a consultant who spent his lifetime savings buying and furnishing a plush beach front office before he learned his product didn't have a market. He could have learned that as easily and less expensively from a spare bedroom.

Knowing yourself

Since succeeding in business will depend primarily on you, you need to be an expert in understanding your strengths and your vulnerabilities. You will need to know if your expectations are realistic. Remember those who start with more modest expectations for success are more likely to succeed.

How are you motivated? Do you need other people to motivate you? Can you work on your own at home?

Do you need a schedule? When do you work best? For example, we find that we begin to run out of steam in the late afternoon, so that's when we do business-related errands.

How do you face problems? Another principle reason for business failure is the failure to face and deal with problems promptly.

What do you do well? What do you need other people to do for you? What skills do you need to improve? Remember, the largest room in the world is the room for self- improvement.

It used to be if you didn't have a business personality it was just too bad. In business, as in almost everything else, as Karl Menninger has said, "Attitude is more important than facts." Today, there are workshops, books and seminars that make it possible for you to develop the personal strengths and skills to succeed in a business of your choice. Today you just need to be honest with yourself and willing to learn.

Knowing how to get help

The survey of successful businesses showed you don't have to do everything yourself. Be willing to use professional advisers, such as lawyers, accountants and consultants. Affiliate with associates. Develop support networks and find partners with personal resources and assets that complement yours.

Remember, even with the divorce rate running at 50%, the failure rate among partnerships is even higher. So pick a business partner with care.

CHAPTER 9

REWARDS

As Nancy and Tom Nickle found in starting N2 Data Serv, you are the key to how much money you can expect to make. "This business can get as big as we want. We've got to decide if we're going to expand or not, hire others, move out of the house or not."

Your earnings can range from a little money on the side to a substantial income. How much you will be able to make will depend upon how much time and energy you invest. It will also depend on whether there is a market for your

---

business, how well you manage the business and how long you persist.

To Barbara Elman one of the greatest rewards of starting her word processing business was the direct reward she got for her own productivity. "In your own business your income is a measure of the amount of business you can generate. Often in an office job the amount of money you make has no relationship at all to what you produce.

"As a secretary I did all my work in record time and then sat for hours doing nothing. I got paid the same no matter how much I worked. My business gives me an instant measure of my productivity and efforts. If I get the work and do it, I get paid."

Norm Goode expressed something worth remembering, "When you've drained the bank account on a display ad that won't appear for three months, success lies in a single word, persistence."

Tax benefits in business

You can get help from Uncle Same at tax time if you use your computer in a business. You must qualify under the tax rules, but if you create a business based on your computer and it produces a profit, you should have no trouble qualifying. The higher your tax bracket, the more you can save.

To pass Uncle Sam's scrutiny, your business must be more than a hobby. IRS considers activities that don't produce a profit at least three years out of five to be hobbies. This lets you take advantage of the tax deductions at the time you are starting up and less likely to make a profit.

You can deduct the cost of your computer in several ways. First, you have the option of taking a capital expense deduction of up to $10,000. This amount should make the entire cost of most personal computer systems deductible in one year. This will be attractive if your income is high during the year you buy your computer.

You can also depreciate your system over a number of years and take an investment tax credit the first year. If you are expecting your income to rise in future years, you may want to spread out the deductions by using depreciation.

If you use your computer for both business and personal non-business uses, such as for entertainment for you or your children, then you can deduct only the portion of your computer investment connected with business.

If you use the computer 75% of the time for business and 25% for pleasure, then you can deduct 75% of the system cost. If you mix the use of your computer, you will need to keep a log to prove how much your computer was used for business.

The cost of business software programs is also deductible. Programs costing less than $100 can be taken as a regular business deduction while programs costing more will need to be treated as a capital expense deduction or depreciated.

Enjoying the benefits

We've asked people who have attended our speeches or entered the Working from Home Forum on CompuServe why they came. Here's some of the things they've said:

"I want to pay for my computer."

"I'm tired of the rat race...I'm fed up with 9 to 5."

"I want to set my own hours and keep what I earn for myself."

"I'm ready to steer my own ship."

"I want to make more money than I'm ever going to make on my job."

"I've been told 'It's none of your business.' so often that I think I'll start my own business."

As you have seen in comments throughout this chapter from people who have done it, turning your computer into a business is not a get rich quick scheme but a means to achieve financial and personal goals.

Starting a business is hard work, but it can be rewarding. You can attain financial, tax and personal benefits.

Personal satisfaction

Personal satisfaction seems to take the benefit prize in this business. As Computer Consultant Bill Slavin put it, "Being an entrepreneur is a thrill!" There's nothing like being your own boss. As Norm Goode describes it, "The joy of creating something of your own from nothing and having it accepted by others is simply beyond words."

Research even shows that working from home on your own is less stressful and thereby better for your health. It can even be good for your relationships. Couples like Nancy and Tom Nickle find they can spend more time together and enjoy sharing their work.

Gil Gordon prizes the family time his new business makes possible. "I'm able to be involved with my kids. We just had a baby and I'm able to be there when I'm needed. I can get involved in things other fathers can't do so easily like going on a nursery school field trip. Sounds a little silly, maybe, but these are precious years everyone tells me go by far too quickly."

It's not all fun. It's not easy, but we find our lives are enriched and agree with Sue Rugge, "As you travel down this path, discomfort is sometimes a companion, though seldom for extensive periods. On the other side of discomfort you will discover a new high that comes with a deeper sense of your own worth. To me, that is the bottom line."

BON VOYAGE

You now know more about the many opportunities that are open to you for starting a business with a personal computer. You know what you will need to do, where to start and where you can turn for help.

Now is just the beginning. Regardless of your talents or interests, there are many profitable opportunities awaiting you. You can join the over 26 million other people who are now self-employed either full or part time. These people may work harder but they experience a greater sense of freedom, accomplishment and satisfaction.

Whatever you're thinking about doing, now is the time to begin. In times like these, someone is going to see the opportunity. Someone's going to have the idea. Someone's going to do it. It might as well be you!

RESOURCES

Books

Computer Entrepreneur, R. H. Morrison, P.O. Box 25130, Honolulu, HI 96825. (800) 528-3665

Skills for Success, Adele Scheele, William Morrow and Company, Inc., N.Y., 1979

Make Money by Moonlighting, Jack Lander, Enterprise Publishing, Inc., Wilmington, DE 19801, 1982

Positioning, the Battle for Your Mind, Al Reis & Jack Trout, Warner Books, N.Y., 1981

Information for Sale: How to Start and Operate Your Own Data Research Service, John Everett and Elizabeth Crowe, 1988

Silicon Valley Guide to Financial Success in Software, Daniel Remer, Paul Remer, Robert Dunaway, Microsoft Press, 1984

A Whack on the Side of the Head - How to Unlock Your Mind for Innovation, Roger von Oech, Warner Books, N.Y., 1983.

References & Directories

Apple Vertical Market Business Directory, Redgate Communications Corp., (305) 231-6904

Gale's Encyclopedia of Associations, Gale Research Company

Data Sources, Ziff-Davis Publishing Company, P.O. Box 5845, Cherry Hill, NJ 08034 (609) 354-4999

MENU Software Guide for IBM & Compatible PC's, P.O. Box MENU, Pittsburgh, PA 15241 (800) THE-MENU

MacMENU Software Guide for Macintosh Computers, see previous listing

Publications of the Small Business Administration. Write for a list of publications: The Small Business Administration, Box 15434, Fort Worth, TX 76119, (800) 433-7272

Direct Mail List Rates and Data, Standard Rate and Data, 5210 Old Orchard Road, Skokie, IL 60076, 800-323-4588

Directory of United States Trade Shows, Expositions and Conventions, The U.S. Travel Service, U.S. Department of Commerce, Washington D.C. 20230.

Magazines and Newsletters

Home Office Computing, PO Box 51344, Boulder, CO 80321

National Home Business Report, PO Box 2137, Naperville, IL. 60566.

Online Services

CompuServe Information Service, 5000 Arlington Centre Blvd., Columbus, OH, 43220 (800) 848-8199. Working from Home Forum. Enter "GO WORK"

Dialog Information Services, 3460 Hillview Avenue, Palo Alto, CA 94304 (415)852-3901

Mead Data Central, 9393 Springboro Pike, P.O. Box 933, Dayton, OH 45401. (800) 227-4908. Full-text legal, medical, business, general.

SECTION 2

BUYING YOUR COMPUTER

CHAPTER 10

KNOWING YOUR COMPUTER NEEDS

Since you'll be using a computer in your business, you'll need to select and master the computer that is best for you. Too many people buy a computer they hear about on television with dreams of starting a business only to discover that the computer can't do what they need. Others are sold on a more expensive computer with more capability and complexity than they can use.

This happened to a friend of ours who wanted "the best." She bought a computer more suited to a large business. The expense was considerable and today it sits unused in her back storeroom. Being a one-person office, she has never had the time to master using it.

If you don't know much about computers, you will need to gain computer literacy. You will need to be knowledgeable in applying the computer to your particular business. Equally important, you'll need to project the self-confidence that comes with knowing what you're doing.

You probably will not need to know how to program. You will better spend the time it would take you learning how to program to learn more business applications of your computer. With the exception of people who work with sophisticated databases that require programming, few businesspeople have a need to program.

To make money with a personal computer, you will need to know how to select and use the software programs, computer system and printer most appropriate for your business. The software tells the computer what to do and enables you to use the computer for business purposes. Throughout this book various software for specific purposes is explained.

Where to find the software you need

To purchase the software that you need, or to find other programs—and please remember that the computer field constantly develops new and better opportunities, you can:

1) Ask for help from your software store. They can direct you to other programs with the features you need.

2) Read announcements of new software and reviews in popular computer magazines such as *Home Office Computing*, *PC Magazine*, *PC Computing*, *InfoWorld*, *PC Week*, *PC World*, *MacUser* and *MacWorld*.

3) Consult software directories such as MENU and Data Sources. They might be found in larger libraries (MENU may be purchased at some software retailers).

4) Use on-line search services. The disadvantage of printed directories is that as fast as the ink dries they are out of date. An on-line search service is a computerized directory that is updated regularly. Examples of such services are found in the MENU on-line service and Dialog's Knowledge Index. Some of these services include evaluation reviews.

5) Hire a consultant to advise you about which software best suits your needs. To locate a consultant, you can get a referral from someone in a similar business to your own or from a computer store. You can also consult Leading Consultants in Computer Software Programming, a directory of over 5000 consultants.

6) Program it yourself. If you have the time, the talent and the desire to custom design your own software, you may find that it not only works for you but can be sold to others with similar needs. (But don't make the mistake of thinking you need to learn to program to learn

to use a computer.)

7) Hire someone to do custom programming for you. You can expect that this will be costly and time consuming. (Refer to the Independent Computer Consultants Association, P.O. Box 27412, St. Louis, MO 63141).

8) Wait. Unless what you are wanting is highly specialized, other businesses will undoubtedly be wanting such a program too. At the rate software is being developed, if it is not available now, it's likely to become available soon.

A final note on software. Don't buy what everyone says is best, unless it is what you need. When you buy, be sure the software comes with a reasonable warranty so that if it doesn't meet your needs, you can exchange it or get your money back. Since software is constantly being updated and improved, get a guarantee that you will be notified of new revisions and have the opportunity to buy them at a reasonable price.

What your computer will need

During our seminars, people frequently ask, "Can any computer make money? Does it make sense to upgrade a 64K home computer to do business?" We think not. You'll spend more money doing this than you would by buying a business computer. Even then you'll still have less, particularly in the area of available software to make your business run effectively.

We have found that there are basic minimum features and characteristics you will want in a business computer as well as important software considerations.

Recommended hardware minimums

We **recom**mend that for business purposes, you need a computer with these minimum characteristics:

1) One floppy disk drive and one hard disk capable of storing a minimum of 40 megabytes of data.

2) A random access memory of 640K, so you can take advantage of current versions of software.

3) At least one serial (RS232) port for communications or a mouse and one parallel port for printing.

4) A keyboard with a separate numeric keypad, separate function keys and separate cursor keys.

5) A monitor. While a monochrome monitor is fine for most work, color is preferred by most people. Of course, it's more expensive.

6) A printer with the appropriate print quality, speed, reliability and serviceability that your business demands.

For business use, we recommend a laser printer, now available for under $1500. A less expensive alternative is an inkjet printer such as Hewlett-Packard's Deskjet Plus now only a few hundred dollars more than a dot matrix printer.

7) Communications capability. While most people wait a year to buy a modem and communications software, we believe that people in business have too much to gain to wait that long. We recommend a fast 2400 baud modem. Such modems are now available for less than $200.

Above and beyond these minimums, you will want to consider the particular features that will help you in your business. You need to consider a color monitor, portability, durability, size limitations and ease of use. Also consider the warranty available on a computer. Many manufacturers offer a twelve month warranty. By purchasing your equipment using some charge cards, you can double your warranty by simply registering it with the credit card company.

Finally take into consideration whether your potential customers will need for you to have a particular kind of computer to be compatible with their computers or their software.

Which type of computer to buy

We do not recommend a home computer, such as the Commodore 64 and 128 or the Radio Shack Color computer for business use. They do not have the capacity or range of software you will want in a business computer.

Usable on airplanes, laptop computers are literally the size of a notebook. The battery operated devices weigh little more than a filled ring binder. Some of the more expensive ones will suffice as your primary business computer, but cheaper ones supplement another computer. They would be excellent, for example, if you do field work and need to have a computer with you. Leading laptop makers include Toshiba, Zenith, Tandy and Compaq.

Greater in size and weight, the desk top computers need a more or less permanent place to sit. These computers are the most common and also have the widest range in price.

IBM compatible computers (MS-DOS) are the most prevalent because they've been around longer, have more software available and are less expensive. In fact, about four out of five home-based businesses use MS-DOS computers. They range from generic "no-name" clones costing well under a thousand dollars to powerhouse computers equivalent to the mainframe computers of not so many years ago.

Today you have a wide range of choices in IBM-compatible computers, in power and speed, brands and places to buy them. For well under a thousand dollars, you can get a "PC" based on the older 8088 microprocessor by mail or in discount warehouses. We recommend you get a computer based on the "286" or "386SX" microprocessor for a home business. Still more powerful computers based on the "386" and "486" microprocessors are for businesses which go beyond word processing in their use of their computer.

Home businesses also use Apple Macintosh computers because of their ease of operation and short learning curve. All Macintosh programs possess a consistent command structure. Once you've learned the commands for your first program, the rest fall into place more readily. Unfortunately, Macintosh computers are more expensive and, for other than the most expensive models, less expandable than MS-DOS computers. There is also less specialized software available for the Macintosh.

For most businesses your choice will be between a desk top and a portable/laptop computer. They should utilize one of the two systems for which most business software is written: an IBM-compatible MS-DOS system or an Apple Macintosh. If budget is not a factor, you may like Apple's Mac II that normally runs Macintosh software but can be made to run MS-DOS software.

To buy now or wait

Many people ask us whether they should wait for prices to come down further, for new technological advances to come on the market or for the "shake out" to take place. We tell them there is no ideal time to buy a computer. Prices will continue to fall and technology will continue to improve indefinitely. The right time to buy is when you are ready to use one. We have found that our computers have paid for themselves many times over and have been worth the investment if they were to be obsolete tomorrow.

In today's market, there is no assurance that any company will remain in business. Just as there were hundreds of makes of automobiles that did not survive, there will be computer companies that won't survive. Buying a computer that consists of standard components and that is sold to many people offers reasonable assurance that service will be available to your system for a long time.

One factor to bear in mind is that if you buy a good computer and the software that you need it will continue to meet your needs even if the manufacturer goes out of business. As long as there is a large installed base of users, there will always be new software and people to repair it.

If you've already bought your computer

If your computer has the capacity to meet the demands of your business and the software you need is available for it, you're in luck. If not, you will need to determine if your computer can be upgraded to do what you need at a reasonable cost. If it can't, you're faced with deciding whether to get a new one. We've come to look at computers like automobiles. If you've been driving a sports coup and add a new member to your family, chances are you'll get a bigger car, and the same applies to computers. If your needs change, your computer may need to change also.

The printer you will need

In business the printer you select for your computer is most important. You send out correspondence, use mailing lists, develop financial records and much more. You may spend as little as $200 for a dot-matrix printer to many thousands of dollars for a laser printer that produces near typeset-quality printing. We've already mentioned the four most important factors in picking a printer as being print quality, speed and reliability and serviceability.

Five key factors to consider in choosing a printer

1) Print quality — whether what's printed looks as if it was typeset or produced by a computer. Documents that look as if they are typewriter-produced are called "letter-quality."

2) Speed — how long it takes to print your work. Printer speeds may be as slow as 11 characters per second for an older-style daisy wheel printer which is about the speed of a fast typist, to over ten pages per minute.

3) Reliability — how long a printer will work before breaking down. Printers are rated in terms of mean time between failures. In considering printers, find out their reputation for reliability.

4) Serviceability — how long it will take to get a printer repaired. You may be able to get your printer repaired on a walk-in basis or you may have to ship it somewhere, leaving you without your printer for weeks. For example, the owner of a high quality printer left a recent message on an electronic bulletin board on

CompuServe Information Service. He expressed his frustration at having to ship his printer to a repair facility in a distant city. He had been without it for five weeks.

5) Noise — in a home office, a noisy impact printer can be more than an irritant; it can lessen your productivity.

How to learn to use your computer and software

Of course, if you don't already know how to use your equipment and software, you'll need to master the operations. You'll want to learn to do this as quickly and easily as possible. Here's what we suggest.

First recognize that you need to devote some time and energy to learning how to use your computer. The amount of time and energy people need varies according to the complexity of the software and your learning style, anywhere from a few hours to a few weeks.

There is not any one answer for everyone. Select an approach that is best suited to your personality, whether it's learning on your own or learning in a classroom.

When considering your computer, if you have no familiarity with using one, remember that the Macintosh is much easier to learn.

Five ways to learn to use your computer

1) If you like to figure things out yourself and you don't mind making mistakes and feeling confused, you can teach yourself using the man-

uals that come with your computer and your software.

2) If you want more assistance than what's available in the manuals, you can buy books and audio and video cassette tapes. They teach you how to use your computer and software. You can find these books and tapes at book stores and software stores, order them by mail through computer magazines or buy them at computer shows.

3) If you like to learn by yourself at your own time and convenience but you've never been good at reading instructions and tinkering around, you can learn in your office or home with tutorial software. Tutorial software enables the computer itself to teach you step-by-step. Since tutorial software is not available for all computers or all software, if you prefer this method of learning, you will want to select a system and software that offers this feature.

4) If you learn better from a live human being, commercial computer schools, computer stores and local colleges and universities all offer computer classes. Talk to the instructor before you sign up to be sure that he or she knows about your computer and about using it in your business. Also be sure the instructor speaks English, not "Computerese." It pays to learn whether you feel comfortable with the instructor and their approach before enrolling.

5) For more personalized assistance hire a consultant or tutor or enlist a friend who has your system and can show you how to begin.

Where to turn for help

If you have problems mastering your computer, there are some additional sources of help such as your computer's manufacturer. Some hardware and software companies now offer 24-hour a day, seven-day-a-week telephone help lines to answer your questions and help you solve problems. Sometimes this support is free, sometimes you must pay for it.

User groups are clubs that can be an excellent source of free help. To locate the computer clubs in your area, ask at local computer stores.

Many software and hardware companies offer users help through CompuServe and other electronic forums devoted to the products of the company. Personally, we have found these sources of help usually more useful and immediate than telephone support. You can almost always find someone who can answer you questions. In fact you may get several answers, but the answers may not all be the same.

Some computer stores offer training, support and assistance. Discount stores and other outlets generally do not. If you are new to computers, we recommend buying from a dealer who provides this service.

Magazines and newsletters are published for all levels of users. They are full of tips and valuable information.

SECTION 3

FINANCING
YOUR BUSINESS

CHAPTER 11

TRAPS
TO AVOID

1. Not having enough money to start up and operate.

2. Not enough money to grow — a problem of success.

3. Too much debt.

4. Cash flow problems.

5. Inadequate financial planning.

6. Not making enough profit to justify the effort or overlooking the risk return tradeoff.

7. Poor credit and collection practices.

8. Inadequate bookkeeping.

CHAPTER 12

SEVEN RULES OF THUMB FOR SUCCESSFUL FINANCE

Rule Of Thumb #1: Start small

Unless you're well established in your field, try to keep your start-up expenses under $5000, including the cost of your computer system. If you can start your business for less, do so. This means using your brain instead of your checkbook.

Anticipate your startup costs and keep them as low as possible. Avoid frills. If in doubt about a major expense item, ask yourself and people whose business advice you can trust, "What would happen if you didn't spend for this now?"

Realistically answering this question may delay your buying a computer with more bells and whistles than you need, delay your incorporating and keep you from opening a plush downtown office.

Typical startup expenses include your computer, software and printer, stationery including design and supplies, business licenses, permits and filings, and other essential equipment and furniture. Other costs include insurance, legal, accounting and consulting fees, telephone installation and deposit fees, and advertising and promotion costs. Still other potential costs are dues and publications, remodeling costs, inventory, and working or operating capital so you can pay bills while you are waiting for income to come in.

If yours is a full-time business, you'll also need to cover the costs of your personal living expenses until you break even.

Most of the successful computer entrepreneurs we talked with kept their start-up costs as low as possible. Sue Rugge and her partner contributed $250 each to start what became Information on Demand. Gil Gordon started his firm for around $6,000 including the cost of his equipment.

Norm Goode started the MicroMoonlighter Newsletter literally on a shoestring. "I believe starting small is important in a start-up business. I took $5,000 of my own savings. I used about $3,000 for the computer, printer and software and invested the rest frugally to start the business. It was money I was willing to gamble and lose. By investing only what you are prepared to lose, you can withstand adverse conditions."

Rule Of Thumb #2: If you have a job, keep it

Remember "The First Rule of Wing Walking"— never let go of something until you've got hold of something else. A new business is always an experiment. Don't give up your current source of income until you know whether your new business is going to take off and whether you like being in business.

Rule Of Thumb #3: Develop an entry plan

Plan how you're going to move from being supported by your current sources of income to being supported by your business. Your goal is for your business to survive that first year. The first year is like the golden hour in emergency medical care.

You can figure it takes 6 months to do anything. We've known of exceptional businesses which produce a profit after 3 months, but most businesses take longer to break even. As Elizabeth Scott and Lucy Ewell forcefully told us, "Everything takes three times longer than you plan." Remember the study of success in small business showed that successful owners had modest expectations. So balance patience with judgment.

Four types of entry plans:

The Moonlighting Plan.

Develop your business as a sideline. When it takes off, you can go full time if you want. Newsletter publishers often begin this way. When they have sufficient subscriptions and advertising, they can make it a full- time business.

The Part-Time Plan.

Work a part-time job to provide a base income while you're building up your business. A musician we know who composes with an electronic synthesizer, for example, is working part-time in a cassette production company while he launches his business. He's not only earning enough to cover his basic expenses, but is also learning valuable technical expertise and making important business contacts.

The Spin-Off Plan.

This approach involves making your employer your first major client or taking a major client with you in situations where this is ethically possible. Computer consultants and programmers often begin this way. When Gil Gordon started his consulting firm he was able to get a retainer from his previous employer to provide a certain amount of work each month.

The Cushion Plan.

With this plan, you have a financial resource to draw on that supports you while you are launching your business. Sabbaticals, divorce settlements, retirement funds, personal savings, an inheritance or a previous investment have launched many a new business venture.

Bill Slavin used personal savings to launch his computer consulting firm. "I had a bonus when I left my job and I had funds from a profit-sharing plan. The biggest surprise I had when the business got going was that I still needed a cushion to fall back on because there is always a germination period between when you start seeking business and when you actually get the work." He found a new business needs about a six month reserve to sustain itself."

Many types of business have to offer credit to their customers to be competitive. If you do, even after you've made the sale and performed the work or provided the good, you will still have to wait to collect any money. Often, as a new business, you will find that you have to pay your suppliers before you can collect from your customers.

Rule Of Thumb #4: Avoid loans and investors

There are three principle sources of financing start-up.

> You can use your own funds.
> You can find investors.
> Or you can borrow.

We advise against using investors or borrowing until you know whether the business is a winner. Then you can use these resources for expansion. We advise this approach because it's difficult to find investors for very small start-up businesses and you won't be able to get a commercial loan for a start-up. As many a disappointed borrower has lamented, "Banks make loans to people who don't need the money."

Michael Anderson used this approach in starting Broadmoor Computer Systems. "I was working out of the house, keeping expenses to a minimum. After I knew the idea was going to work out, I got investors from the family and eventually a bank loan. Banks are looking at you to see that you can do it."

Bill Slavin agrees, "I didn't consider outside financing until recently when I realized that after three years of business I need to finance the growth of the firm."

So while you may be able to borrow money from relatives, friends or by using your personal assets as security, borrowing adds to the expense of operating your business. It puts you under additional financial pressure. It is better to start small and use the income your new business brings in to engage in what is called "bootstrap" financing." Bootstrap financing is the essence of effective cash flow management which we'll discuss in a moment.

Rule Of Thumb #5: Finance the start-up yourself

Here are some ideas for how to get funds for start-up costs:

earnings
selling valuables
savings
unemployment compensation
retirement funds
a leave or sabbatical
insurance loans
profits from an existing business
piggy-backing on a spouse's earnings.

Tom and Nancy Nickle piggy-backed their business, living off Tom's salary while they got the business underway. "I'm conservative. I wouldn't have done this if I didn't have a job and could do it without overexposing myself financially. I say ease into it the safe way. Try it out. Get your feet wet taking on a little more and more. Part of our success has been this approach."

Rule Of Thumb #6: Manage your cash flow

Get any two new small business owners together and before long, they'll mention problems with cash flow. It's the classical bane of new businesses. Cash flow to a business is what breath is to life. Here are three basic strategies for managing cash flow wisely:

1. Minimize what other people owe you.
2. Utilize cash on hand for maximum benefit.
3. Hold onto what you have.

Now for some tips on how to capitalize on these strategies to "bootstrap your business" and get it to finance itself:

Get deposits, retainers, partial or progress payments.

Take payment in cash at the time of sale or delivery of service.

Take bank cards instead of extending credit.

When you must bill people, offer discounts of from 2 to 5% for receipt of payment within 10 days from the date of the invoice.

Bill people immediately instead of waiting until the end of the week or the month.

Act promptly on overdue accounts.

If your business is large enough, use the cash management programs of a bank.

Use cash on hand to maximum advantage by depositing it in interest-bearing accounts and using money market funds.

To get and keep your business, some suppliers will give 30, 60, even 90 days of interest free credit. Unfortunately they will often hesitate to offer these terms to a new business.

Use charge cards. You'll get 30 to 60 days free use of money.

Make timely but not immediate payment of bills.

Rent or lease equipment rather than tying up your capital in owning it.

Rule Of Thumb # 7: Price low enough for your market but high enough for you

In pricing, take into account what the competition charges, the value to the customer and the customer's expectations and ability to pay. You also need to consider your costs, which include your time, overhead, materials, supplies and especially your profit goals.

Dorothy Baranski found in operating Dorbar Executive Services that by pricing her word processing and financial management services lower in the beginning, she could raise her rates as her reputation grew. "You may have to start out making less profit to build your reputation. Make sure your overhead is covered first and then add a little bit of money to live on. Since people care most about the quality of your work in a service business, satisfied customers are the best thing you can have. They'll stick with you when you raise your prices because they want 'you' to do their work."

Tom and Nancy Nickle worried about meeting price resistance if they charged for all the costs of programming at the time they began to handle freight billing for a company. They worked out a monthly freight billing charge that prorated the programming fee throughout the year. This pricing strategy enables companies to start the service for a reasonable cost and distributes the Nickles' income more evenly throughout the year.

These are our seven rules of thumb, learned from working with many small businesses and

from starting them ourselves. As you make
your plans for financing your business, you may
want to hire a financial consultant to help you
be sure you are on the right track.

SECTION 4

14 STEPS TO
STARTING YOUR BUSINESS

CHAPTER 13

STEP ONE: LOCATING ADEQUATE OFFICE SPACE

We recommend that you start your business at home if at all possible. This will enable you to keep your start-up costs and operating expenses low while you are building the business. Fortunately, most computer businesses can be run from your home whether it's a house, an apartment or a condominium.

Your personal computer probably won't require any special electrical or environmental modifications. We do recommend, however, that you get a "surge protector" to safeguard against high voltage spikes and electrical noise that can cause you to lose data or change it unpredictably. Sensitive components in you computer can also be destroyed. A surge protector that does the job will cost around $70. If you have difficulty with power outages in your area or with blowing circuit breakers, you should buy software that periodically saves material on your data disks automatically. You may also want to buy a backup power supply device. Prices for such devices begin at around $500.

A separate, clearly defined space set aside only for your business works better in most households. It is also necessary to qualify for a home-office tax deduction. To be believable to the IRS, it used to be said your home-office needed to have enough office space for at least a desk, a chair and a filing cabinet. Today, your desk may be a computer table and your filing cabinet your disk storage.

You may want to acquire specialized computer furniture, designed to handle the special requirements of your system — things like holes for power cords and cables, trays and shelves for components and manuals. Your comfort at the computer is important and computer furniture is designed with this consideration in mind.

In locating your office, you will want to plan for adequate lighting and freedom from glare. We prefer daylight and incandescent lighting.

You should anticipate needing at least 10% of your space for storage. Even with a computer, your files and records will grow.

The most common place for an "electronic cottage" office is a spare bedroom. Usually it's large enough and separate enough from other household activities for you to work comfortably. If you don't have a spare bedroom, here are some ideas of how other small businesses have modified their existing space to accommodate their computer and the business.

They have used a den or family room or a breakfast room, or a closet or a storage area. Often they use their garage or a side porch, attic or basement. A separate building such as a guest house or cabana often makes an ideal location.

If you don't have a suitable separate area, you can create a separate business space by dividing any room with screens, bookcases or furniture. You can enclose a porch or patio, add on a room or even construct a separate building. In fact, we've known someone who set up their business in an RV parked in their side yard.

CHAPTER 14

STEP TWO:
CHECK
ZONING REGULATIONS

If you have your business in your home, you can determine if your home can be used for business by checking the zoning ordinances at either your city hall or county court house. To know whether you need to check with the city or the county, a general rule of thumb is that if you would call the police, you are governed by city zoning; if you phone the sheriff, you deal with the county.

Zoning regulations typically divide communities into residential, commercial, industrial and agricultural zones, with subdivisions within these categories. Even in residential areas, many zoning regulations allow "home occupations" with limitations such as the home being primarily used as a residence, no signs or commercial displays and no "stock in trade" sold on the premises. They may also require there be no employees, machinery or mechanical equipment on the premises.

Most computer-related businesses would not violate these restrictions. In fact, people rarely know you're operating a business.

The most common ways zoning violations are discovered are when your neighbors complain or your business becomes visible because of traffic, parking or noise. Sometimes your city or county is notified when you apply for a business license or for a sales tax resale number, also known as a certificate of authority in some states.

Good neighbor relations are the best asset for avoiding zoning problems.

CHAPTER 15

STEP THREE: DETERMINE THE FORM OF YOUR BUSINESS

In setting up your business you have three basic choices. You can become a sole proprietorship, a partnership or a corporation. (For further information see Section 7, Working With Numbers, page 187.)

We recommend beginning as a sole proprietor unless your business faces the danger of being sued for damages or you've already decided to work with a partner.

You should always consult an attorney and accountant when planning the structure of your business.

CHAPTER 16

STEP FOUR
SELECTING AND
REGISTERING
YOUR BUSINESS NAME

Your business name will be your primary business identity, so select it with both creativity and care. Your business name should be easy to remember, not too short and not too long and simple to spell and pronounce. It should be unique. You don't want to be confused with other businesses. Your name should evoke the business "image" you want to convey to your customers or clients. Names other businesses have chosen are everywhere, on everything you buy and use. Examples of small business names include The MicroMoonlighter Newsletter, Word Processing News, Word Smithing, Letter Perfect, Rising Star Industries, Computer Consultants, Inc., The Computer Coach, Programmers' Pipeline and Rent-To-Own Computers.

The more specific the name, the more clear it is what product or service your business provides. "Letter Perfect" is a word processing service and clearly lets customers know what service it will provide and adds the suggestion of quality. If the owner wants to expand into other areas, however, this name may become limiting. A name such as "Rising Star Industries" doesn't reveal what the high tech research company does. It does allow leeway for the many products the company will develop and conveys a positive image.

We recommend coming up with several alternative names and trying them out with friends and people in your field. Give yourself several days to see which one feels best to you before deciding. Remember you will have to live with your name for some time to come, perhaps even for the rest of your life.

Once you have selected your name, you will need to register and protect it. If you are a sole proprietorship you will need to file a fictitious business name with the Secretary of State or with your local county clerk, depending on state law. If your business is a corporation, you will need to reserve the name with the Secretary of State. You may wish to trademark your name to protect it from use by others. You do this through your state, or if you meet the qualifications, you may register it with the U.S. Patent Office in Washington, D.C. Federal registration takes about 1 year to 18 months and currently costs between $40 and $50.

CHAPTER 17

STEP FIVE
FILING YOUR PAPERWORK

Because state, county and local regulations vary from place to place, you will need to determine if your business requires any of several licenses and permits. These include a city or county license, a state sales permit, a federal employer's identification number or any other special licenses.

Even if you are not required to have one, we recommend that you get an employer's ID number. It will cost nothing, but will convey the image of a substantial business. You can get your Federal ID number from the nearest Internal

---

Revenue Service office.

Knowing the specific licenses you need is an important safeguard against future headaches. We know of a woman who started an electronic housing rental referral only to discover that in her state she needs a real estate license to do that. We also know someone who started a word processing service and conducted business for over a year before the state notified her that she owed sales tax on many of her services. The back taxes nearly put her out of business. So check out your state's requirements before you start.

CHAPTER 18

STEP SIX
CREATING YOUR IMAGE

Business cards and stationery are more than paper you use for correspondence. Think of them as miniature billboards for your business. They create a first impression for people with whom you don't have face to face contact. They tell the world about your business. Some of the people you do business with may only know you through your stationery. Think about your stationery and your business cards as part of your promotion and sales efforts.

Design your logo, cards and stationery to make a statement about your business. Have them convey the "image" you wish to create about your business. For example, if a software firm wants to project a modern "high tech" look, you might use a paper, type style and design that convey a clean, sleek, cool and forward looking image. If you instead want to convey a friendly, safe environment, you may choose a paper, type style and design that is rounded, warm, soft and reminiscent of the familiar past.

Your card and stationery usually include your business name, your name if it's different from that of the business, your logo and your address and phone number.

We recommend at least a 24 pound bond paper for letterhead and stationery and 60 to 70 pound stock for business cards. The type should be large enough to be easily read, especially the telephone number. Since typesetters usually make the phone number too small, specify at least 10 point type and place the number in the lower right hand corner of your card. That is where people's eyes come to rest.

Shopping wisely can keep costs to $200. For low cost design work, approach local schools of design for students to design your logo. You can use only one color of ink, but don't skimp on paper. The money you save is minimal. Printing in quantities of 1000 often costs only slightly more than printing 500. On the other hand, don't go overboard until you know what you have printed is effective. We know a man with 2,000 purple brochures in his garage.

CHAPTER 19

STEP SEVEN
DEVELOPING
YOUR BUSINESS PLAN

A business plan is the road map for your business. It sets out your goals, where you're going in your business and how you plan to get there. Beyond being a necessity for finding investors or getting a loan, a business plan is primarily for you. It helps you be realistic about turning your dreams into reality and helps you avoid surprises and failures.

To develop your business plan, answer these questions:

What is your business? Describe it in 65 words or less and write it so that a 10 year old can understand it.

Who are your intended customers or clients?

Why do you think they need what your business offers?

How are you going to get their business?

How will they know about what you can do for them?

How much money do you need before you open?

What are your operating costs going to be?

How are you going to price your goods or services?

How much can you sell?

How long will it be before your sales will cover your costs?

How long before you'll make a profit?

How are you going to pay your bills in the meantime?

A business plan answers these basic questions. Writing one does not have to be a complicated or difficult process. If you follow Jack Lander's advice in his book *Make Money by Moonlighting* you can write your business plan in the form of a personal letter to a friend. Here's an example:

"Dear Friends,

You'll remember all those mail order magazines I had stacked up by the computer in my spare bedroom. Well, I'm finally going to start my own mail order business. I've developed a manual for how to use the computer information services easily and simply. Projections indicate that 25 per cent of American homes will have computers by 1990. Already over 200,000 computer owners have a modem and belong to at least one communications service. This number is growing rapidly.

I've joined several major on-line services and have learned to use them successfully. That's not always easy. I know the difficulties a novice can have, because I had them myself and I have interviewed close to 50 people who have tried to use a service for the first time. With this knowledge I developed a desk reference guide on how to use the services and had it printed. I've got 2000 copies overflowing the closet and ready to go in the mail.

I've been to the book stores and the computer stores so I know that there is nothing out like what I've got to offer. I've also set my price at just below the average price of the most popular computer books.

I'm going to start by advertising in computer magazines. I've picked out those with the largest circulations, and I plan to submit articles on computer networking to these magazines and to send news releases.

I figure if I sell 25 guides it will pay for the ad and after I've sold 273 I will have paid for producing these products. After that I'll be making a profit.

The display ad will be the most important variable. I've taken a class on writing mail order display ads and I think I have one that will draw. I'll be able to identify which magazine is pulling in the most orders by coding the return addresses. So I'll soon know if my strategy will work.

If it does, there probably won't be room for any overnight guests because between the computer and the guides, I'll be selling the bed. If all goes well, we'll be adding that extra room on to the house that Bill and I have wanted for so long.

Wish me luck,

Signed "Nan of The Networks."

CHAPTER 20

STEP EIGHT
MEETING YOUR BANKER

You will need to set up a separate business checking account for your new business. We recommend selecting a small or a local neighborhood bank where your business will be noticed and valued.

If you are happy with your existing bank, you may want to open your business account there because you already have a good relationship.

Find out what the bank's policy is on holding checks deposited for collection. Some banks won't credit your account for checks until they have cleared if the checks are above a certain amount or if they fail to meet other criteria. Accept only immediate use of your funds.

Get to know and have a friendly relationship with all the bank employees. You never know when that may become important. We're always surprised by how little favors can make a difference.

CHAPTER 21

STEP NINE
SETTING UP
YOUR BOOKKEEPING

The purpose of keeping good records is to enable you to know how your business is doing. You'll learn where you are making a profit and where you aren't. It'll illustrate what your costs have been, what areas you can cut expenses in and what ways you will need to modify your plans and projections. It will enable you to pay the minimum legal taxes you owe and protect you should you be audited.

Your goal should be to keep simple, accurate records. If you wish to hire a bookkeeping service, prices in each area vary. In our area, the cost currently runs around $20 an hour or $75 a month for basic bookkeeping and tax reporting records. You can consider locating an electronic bookkeeping service compatible with your computer system.

Two valuable resources are the Internal Revenue Service Publication 334, a Tax Guide for Small Business and a Small Business Administration publication, Keeping Records in Small Business, number MA 1.017. The latter is one of many free or low cost publications available from the Small Business Administration.

CHAPTER 22

STEP TEN
GETTING YOUR
EQUIPMENT AND SUPPLIES

We suggest that you generate a list of what minimal things you expect you will need. A good way to start if you are currently working at a job is to go through your office desk. Write down a list of what you find on top of and in the drawers. If you have a secretary, find out and list the common office supplies she keeps on hand.

A typical list will include file folders, paper clips, a calendar, staple remover, appointment book, glue, rubber cement, address book or Rolodex, rubber bands, pens, pencils, erasers, hi-liters, letter opener, tape, in and out box, rubber stamp, paper cutter, check protector, pencil holder, envelopes, paper weight, index cards, stamps, paper cutter, postage meter, postage affixer, scissors, floppy disks, ruler, disk cleaning kit, stapler, printer paper, file tabs, large envelopes, jiffy bags....

CHAPTER 23

STEP ELEVEN
SETTING UP
YOUR TELEPHONES

If you are working from your home, you often do not have to get a separate business phone unless you want a yellow page listing. Using residential lines helps keep your costs down.

You may wish to get another residential line, however, so you can have an incoming and outgoing line or a business and a personal line.

If you want a business listing but would like to save the several hundred dollar deposit required to install a business line, install a new residential line. Then once it's installed, call the phone company and ask to have your new residential line changed to a business line.

We recommend getting touch tone phones for convenience and electronic communications. We suggest you buy your phones. If you buy a good one that will hold up, it will pay for itself in a year. Our experience is that phones made in the United States are more durable.

You'll want to arrange for an answering service or an answering machine to take your calls when you are away or when you don't want to take business calls.

The choice between an answering machine and an answering service is one of personal preference. Answering services provide a live person to answer your phone. They are less aggravating than answering machines to many people and they may communicate more prestige. On the other hand, they tend to answer slowly, leave unclear messages or give your messages to someone else and they're notorious for being rude and abrupt.

Answering machines cost less. They leave a reliable message and offer your own personal greeting. However, many people dislike them, and some will hang up when they hear an answering machine. They are also subject to occasional mechanical failure. Today, however, people are becoming more sophisticated about answering machines and we're noticing a smaller percentage of people are hanging up. In case you haven't guessed, we have an answering machine.

Prices vary by location. In our area, the lowest price we've found for an answering service is about $40 per month for service from 9 to 5, Monday through Friday. We have heard that computerized answering services are more reliable. An answering machine that will serve your business needs will cost between $125 and $300, depending on the features you select. If you are away from your office and need to check your calls, for example, you can get an answering machine with remote playback. You can then phone in to retrieve your messages.

If your business will involve extensive long-distance calling you may want to subscribe to a lower-cost long- distance service. If you have over $25 of long-distance costs a month, you should consider this option. Check the services in your area and select the one with the best rates and the clearest telephone lines.

CHAPTER 24

STEP TWELVE
SETTING UP
YOUR MAIL SERVICE

If you are working from your home, you probably will not need to do anything special about your mail service. We have checked this with the Postal Service and they have told us there is no problem with delivering business mail to a residential address in any amount. However, you may need to get a bigger mailbox.

If you fear giving your home address as your business address will hurt your image, par-

---

ticularly because you live on Easy Street or Sleep Hollow Lane, get a post office box. You can also rent an address from a private mail receiving service.

CHAPTER 25

STEP THIRTEEN
GETTING INSURANCE

If you are working from home, you will want to get a business rider on your homeowners insurance to cover liability to business visitors coming into your home. This business endorsement will cost approximately $10 a year. If you have employees, you may also need Workers' Compensation Insurance.

You'll need additional coverage to insure your computer and other business property against loss. Homeowner policies usually don't cover your computer if it's business equipment. Even if you use your computer partly for personal purposes, the business portion isn't covered without buying additional coverage.

If you'll be taking your computer out of the house, you may need to get separate insurance coverage to protect it from loss or damage. We found that once our computer was out of the house, it wasn't covered either by the business coverage we added to our homeowners policy or our automobile insurance. Companies offering special computer insurance include Columbia National General Agency, Inc. in Columbus, Ohio; Data Security Insurance Agency in Boulder, Colorado; and Personal Computer Insurance Agency in San Jose, California. Some companies offer policies covering the cost of reconstructing lost data files.

CHAPTER 26

STEP 14
ESTABLISHING
YOUR WORK SCHEDULE

Keep a work schedule. It will not only help you organize your work, but will help family and friends know when they can and cannot interrupt you. Business contacts will also get to know when it's best to reach you. A schedule will even help you to avoid having your work take over your life as it is apt to do when you own your own business.

If you are operating a part-time business, we have some suggested time guidelines. Plan to work at least 8 hours a week at a minimum. Plan to spread the 8 hours out throughout the week so that you are not waiting to squeeze it all into the weekend. This way when something you want to do or have to do arises on weekends, you can still get work done that week.

Avoid scheduling work during important personal time like Monday night football or your favorite club night. Work no more than 11 months of the year. You'll need a month off. We've found that adhering to these few guidelines will not only keep you productive, but also healthy.

We've discovered a few other rules of thumb. When you are working, work as though you were at a regular office. You'll probably find you are more productive because of the absence of office politics. Set goals for what you want to accomplish each day or week. Keep track of how you're spending your time. Use "To Do" lists and a system to set priorities for what to do first. We've developed "The Time Manager," a one-page daily planner, to help ourselves and others manage time more effectively.

CHAPTER 27

WHERE TO GET HELP

Beyond learning these 14 Start-Up Steps you may need to take courses or read some of the many books on starting your own business. Pay particular attention to those featuring areas about which you know the least. The Small Business Administration offers free or low cost business courses in most communities. Local colleges and universities offer business courses in their extension programs.

There are many good books on starting a business. A popular one is Paul Hawken's *Growing a Business*. An excellent magazine for keeping up with income opportunities using your computer is *Home Office Computing*, for which we write a the monthly column, "Working Smarter," focusing on home-based business. The entire magazine discusses sales and marketing ideas, trends, resources and the in's and out's of specific businesses.

SECTION 5

PROMOTING
YOUR BUSINESS

CHAPTER 28

FREE PUBLICITY

Author Jack Lander claims that square inch for square inch, free publicity is more effective than paid advertising. That certainly has been our experience. In a sense, it isn't free. You have to qualify for it by being newsworthy. You also have to spend the time and money to contact the media either yourself or by hiring a publicist or public relations firm to do it for you.

Public Relations consultant Michael Baybeck suggests you set aside a specific amount of time for "PR." He suggests five hours a week. He advises treating PR as an investment account. You send out a news release a month, make five PR oriented phone calls a week and have at least one PR lunch a month.

Being newsworthy

To get free publicity you have to become "newsworthy." You have to have something to say or offer that is different and of interest to others. The fact that Susan Smith is starting a word processing service on 10th Street isn't particularly newsworthy. If Susan's new business opens announcing the results of a survey she conducted showing word processing cuts mailing list costs in half, that could be newsworthy. Armed with this survey she'll have a much better chance of getting news coverage.

Sometimes great publicity comes from taking advantage of opportunity. Joseph Cossman, author of the book, *How I Made a Million Dollars in Mail Order*, and an expert at self- promotion, once found a mallard duck in his swimming pool. He called the local newspaper and TV station, who covered the story. The newspaper syndicated the story nationally and in each story appeared the identification of Cossman as the author of *How I Made a Million Dollars in Mail Order*. Not bad for a phone call.

News releases

To reach your particular market, it's not just what you say but where you say it. You can get your message out to prospective customers through trade and professional publications, newsletters, magazines and business, as well as general interest, newspapers by sending news releases that lead to product reviews or an announcement about your business.

News releases are usually 1 to 2 page statements of newsworthy events. They can announce a new product, release the results of a survey or report on an upcoming promotional event such as an all-day computer demonstration at a local shopping center.

Interviews

News releases or calls to local radio, TV and print media can lead to appearances on TV or radio talk shows or to feature articles about you and your business. Today everyone is interested in computers. If you are doing something new and different with your computer or can tell others how they can do something new and different with their computer you could be swamped with invitations.

When Elizabeth Scott and Lucy Ewell began writing software for girls, their message was different. They were saying that girls approach computer games differently than boys, and that if girls don't get involved in computers, their future will be limited. They have written software that solves these problems. These discoveries are newsworthy. Educators and people with daughters immediately want to hear about this. It is no wonder they have gotten good coverage.

Writing articles

Getting an article that you have written published establishes you as an expert in your field. To get an article published, send it to publications whose subscribers are potential customers or clients or send a query letter describing an article you could write. Remember to include your photo, a biographical sketch and your address and phone number for the box describing the author.

Telecommuting (working at home while being employed by a company) is a new phenomenon. Gil Gordon knew he would have to educate the corporate market to its benefits if he was going to get hired to develop pilot telecommuting projects. He began writing articles for business magazines, describing the benefits and problems of telecommuting. These articles have helped to establish him as an authority in an emerging field.

Contacting new product editors

Having a respected magazine or newsletter recommend your product is much more valuable than advertising you do yourself. Many periodicals have a new products section in which they review products and services they think will be of value to their readers. When Bernard Husbands personally contacted computer magazines to promote Programmers' Pipeline, the novelty of his service enabled it to be featured by several of them. Recently he got 45 to 50 inquiries from one article.

This approach is particularly good when targeted to publications your prospective customers read. For example, when we produced our cassettes on "How to Start a Word Processing Service" with Barbara Elman, we sent news releases and sample tapes to influential computer business newsletters. They reviewed the tapes and we got orders as a result. In addition we were able to use quotations from the reviews in further publicizing the tapes. We use reprints of the reviews and can say in describing the product, "as reviewed in so and so's newsletter."

Teaching courses and seminars

Adult education is growing 35% a year. There are lots of opportunities to offer courses in college continuing education programs, adult education organizations, churches, YMCA's and department stores. While teaching classes or seminars you can meet many prospective clients as well as attract wholesalers, reps or other contacts that can help your business.

Computer consultants often teach free or fee classes on selecting a business computer as a way to reach prospective clients.

Freelance programmer, Jim Milburn finds he doesn't need to advertise for business because he generates all the business he needs from the programming classes he teaches at a computer training school.

Writing a book, chapter or pamphlet on your area of expertise further establishes you as an expert. You can sell the books, use them as promotional items or give them away as incentives for people to buy your product or service. You can also use them to help you get book, radio and TV interviews.

Speaking

You can speak about your services or your product. There are more than 9000 speaking opportunities every day in the United States. Speaking on subjects related to your business is particularly useful for certain services. These include computer schools, camps and consulting services. In these, people like to feel they have a personal relationship with the person they buy from.

One woman started a children's computer learning center in a shopping center where mothers could leave their children while shopping. To promote her new business, she got bookings on radio and TV talking about the importance and problems of children learning to use computers. She spoke at local churches and parent groups. She used tantalizing titles like "Will Your Children Become Arcade Addicts?"

Computer consultant Bill Slavin finds that speaking and leading seminars provide him with the high profile he needs to attract business. He finds, "You never know for sure who will be a potential client in the future. So I've found that you have to treat everyone you meet as a potential client. You can convert the acquaintances you have made at speeches or seminars into clients by contacting them yourself.

You have to follow-up by calling on them, however, or they will think of you as a speaker or seminar leader instead of a consultant."

CHAPTER 29

NETWORKING
THE SECRET TO SUCCESS

"Networking" is the informal process of meeting people who might be able to help you get business. It lets you inform them what you are doing and how they can support your efforts. Sue Rugge, founder of Information on Demand, puts it this way, "Talking to people is the best way to get business." Computer consultant Bill Slavin agrees, "I try to have no lunches alone. If I'm going to have lunch, I try to schedule it with a client or prospective client."

Family networks, of course, are the oldest networks of all. They have long been a boon to business, as have civic, religious and professional organizations. Now electronic networks are becoming popular.

Membership in professional and trade associations is a way to find out what others are doing, what's working, what isn't and where there are "holes in the market." They can lead to affiliations and referrals that benefit your business.

You can also join associations and groups where your potential buyers might gather. For example, if you are wanting to sell computer peripherals to computer owners, go to user group meetings. Unless the meeting sets aside time for sales, don't try to sell there or give your pitch to everyone you meet. Use your time to establish contacts, build relationships, gather information and ask questions. Give people your card, but more important, GET THEIR CARD! Then follow-up with phone contacts.

Today there are network organizations, business guilds and lead clubs whose sole purpose is to help members give and get leads. They usually meet at mealtimes and limit membership to one person in a given kind of business. For example, when Dorothy Baranski opened an executive word processing service, she joined a women's network and a breakfast lead club in her area. She built her business off these two sources of contacts.

Telecommunications consultant Gil Gordon summarizes how networking has worked for him, "Everything in business, whether it's getting an article published or finding a distributor, is a result of networking. I keep in contact with old friends, past co-workers, sales reps who used to call on me. I've joined a couple of carefully chosen small associations or discussion groups composed of the people I need to meet for my business and I'm fortunate enough to know a couple of people who pride themselves on being 'matchmakers.' They love to get people with common interests together. I can't stress this enough. Just as in job- hunting, your friends and contacts are your best assets."

CHAPTER 30

ADVERTISING
MAKING EVERY
DOLLAR COUNT

Advertising not only can get you buyers but can identify wholesalers or retailers as well. They see your ads appearing in trade-related publications month after month. A few buyers or wholesalers may place an order from your ad, but others will be more likely to respond positively to a direct contact after seeing your ad regularly.

Classified and display ads

You can advertise your business in newspapers, magazines or newsletters through either display advertising or classified ads. Display advertising is expensive, but can be worth the investment if properly targeted.

When Elizabeth Scott and Lucy Ewell launched their software company, their primary marketing effort was to take out a full-page color ad in *SoftTalk Magazine*. This was a carefully thought out strategy. They wrote their software games for use on Apple computers by young girls ages 7 to 12. *SoftTalk* was an Apple computer magazine that came free for one year with every Apple computer. The big bright colored ads attracted the interest of girls who might enjoy the games. Response to the ad was highly successful.

Display advertising can be expensive and not a wise per dollar investment for everyone. Many computer entrepreneurs such as Norm Goode of MicroMoonlighter Newsletter begin by taking classified ads in targeted magazines and then placing display ads in those magazines from which response is high.

A woman we met opened an electronic bookkeeping service and took out ads in her local community paper and in a local business tabloid. She got a good response from nearby businesses, the very ones most likely to want her services.

Barbara Elman used a similar approach to get business for her word processing service. "I advertised regularly in the place that reached my particular market, scriptwriters, most directly, the Hollywood trade papers. In the legal field it might be in the local law journal; in the academic field, the university newspaper.

"You don't have to use a big ad. In fact the small ads I ran regularly drew more business than the enormous several hundred dollar ads I ran once. I found that having an ad run regularly and having some kind of logo or copy that was catchy and showed I knew what I was doing drew best. When people suddenly needed typing, they remembered my ad from having seen it 6 months ago. Now, sure enough, there it is today too. They know you are a serious business."

It's tempting to advertise only when you need business but Barbara found this doesn't work. "Advertising only when you need business is only going to bring too much business at once. Then you'll be too busy to take it and have to turn it away. Advertising all the time even when you're busy will bring in the business when you need it most — at the slower periods."

To save costs, she recommends looking at the peaks and valleys of your particular area and market. In the academic market, for example, summer is slow, while final exam time is high. In Barbara's business, scriptwriters were busy most of the year but Thanksgiving to New Years is slow. Following this pattern, you can advertise more during the peaks and cut back during the valleys.

Exchanging advertising for articles or columns you write

Another way to keep your advertising costs down is to write an article or column in exchange for advertising. Small or new publications not only have better prices but are often willing to give you advertising space in exchange for writing articles or a column. Watch for announcements of new publications.

CHAPTER 31

STILL MORE IDEAS

Drop shipping

Newsletters or catalogs may be willing to sell your product themselves, usually on a drop ship basis. They take a percentage of the sale and forward you a check for the balance and the cost of mailing. Then you ship the products directly to the buyer, and in the course of that build your own mailing list.

Computer and cable television opportunities

Bulletin boards on computer services and cable television offer low or no-cost ways of reaching a generally "upscale" market. Making your own television shows by taking advantage of "public access programming" can get you local exposure and give you television experience. To find out about cable television possibilities, visit the offices of your local cable operator.

There are both local and national computer bulletin boards. To learn about local boards, ask about them at computer stores and at user group meetings. To use the national services such as CompuServe, Source and Delphi, you will need to subscribe. We operate the Working From Home Forum on CompuServe through which people regularly make useful business connections and gain valuable information.

Fliers and tear-off pads

A simple way to reach buyers if your market is limited to a particular geographic area is to use fliers or tear-off pads. If you are providing word processing services for a college campus market, for example, you can announce your services on fliers. You can mount them on bulletin boards or hand them out at events where people gather.

You can place a tear-off pad on local bulletin boards so that interested customers can tear off a slip good for a 10% discount with your name and telephone number. To help pay for the purchase of their computer, we've had people in our seminars decide to do computer tutoring, teaching other people how to begin using their newly purchased computers. One person placed a tear pad on the bulletin board at a local computer store. The store offered two free hours of training to each new buyer, but many buyers were wanting more attention. The store was happy to have somewhere to refer them.

Using Newsletters

A consultant learned the hard way that large, expensive direct mail campaigns produce a low return on the dollar. Following the advice of Howard Shenson, who is known as "the consultant's consultant," he switched to publishing a newsletter for prospective clients. He found, as Shenson had predicted, that newsletters don't get tossed in the trash but get read. His business increased.

You can use your computer for desktop publishing to print a newsletter yourself without many headaches or costs. If you want the newsletter professionally printed, you can locate an electronic printing service. By entering the proper commands into your copy, you can even send it directly to the printer via your modem.

Howard Shenson has a three-hour audio cassette series on "How to Start and Promote Your Own Newsletter" which is available through his newsletter, *The Professional Consultant*.

Getting no-cost high-quality help on your promotional material

To get free feedback on the effectiveness of your promotional material, Howard Shenson suggests you contact a faculty member in the marketing department of a university school of business. College professors are always wanting "real world" examples for their classes. Explain that you would like ideas on your marketing campaign. Bring your brochures and material to the class. You'll get plenty of feedback and ideas, maybe even more than you expect.

Personal letters and thank you notes

Computer consultant Bill Slavin prefers writing personal letters to prospective clients. "I could never isolate a job where the client was attracted to the firm by a brochure. A brochure is something to assure that your name is in someone's file. So instead of using brochures, I focus on personal mailings. I write letters to the people I want to talk to, trying to provide value in the letter, addressing to the extent possible the particular problems they have and offering ways they might solve their special problems."

Steve Maier, who sells sales training in the computer field, has found that simple thank you notes he writes to follow-up on contacts generate enough business to pay his $5,000 annual printing bill.

CHAPTER 32

MEETING THE WORLD TRADE SHOWS

Another way of reaching customers is at trade shows. It's not unusual for a computer show, for example, to attract from 20,000 to 100,000 people. You can actually sell products at many of these shows.

Computer author Carol Dysart reports excellent results selling her books and products while speaking at computer shows. Besides attracting customers, however, trade shows are good avenues for reaching retailers, wholesalers, reps and buyers. Exhibiting is also a good way to test a new product, build your mailing list and conduct informal market surveys.

If you haven't exhibited before, attend some shows in your market area first. Ask those who have booths if they feel it has been worth their while. See if any exhibitors are interested in carrying your product or are selling services similar to yours.

You can find out about trade shows through the Directory of United States Trade Shows, Expositions and Conventions, which is available at some libraries.

If you want to sell at a show, we think you'll do better at smaller, regional shows where there's an admission fee and the attendees have paid their own way.

A moonlighter from one of our courses launched his line of computer-chip jewelry at a gift show. He booked over $10,000 of orders from gift shops. An independent publisher attended the American Bookseller's Association convention with her newly published book on word processing and launched the book.

CHAPTER 33

CLOSE ENCOUNTERS
WITH PERSONAL SELLING

Personal selling has a role in any business. In fact, as you can see from the approaches we've described so far, you will be selling yourself, your product and your business everywhere you go. Basic selling skills are a must. If this is not one of your skills, as is the case with many of us, we urge you to take some sales courses. After all, no doctor ever looked at a newborn baby and said, "Now, here's a natural-born salesman."

The President of Broadmoor Computer Systems, Michael Anderson attributes much of his success to experiences he had in college that taught him the basic skills of selling. "I was involved with the International Association of Students in Business & Marketing and participated in placing foreign students in internships with American companies. I learned not to be afraid to present myself and to talk to people. I learned that if I knew my facts people would respect me. The experience taught me how to interview, ask questions and listen. I've found that life, and particularly business, is nothing more than a series of interviews."

Although selling will be part of everything you do, some businesses find that direct selling is the best avenue to get business. When a retired sales manager decided to repair computers for small businesses, he got started by going through the yellow pages. He called on companies to determine if they needed his services.

Telephone sales can be an important sales aid. A husband and wife started a computer consulting practice. To make contacts, they decided to hold low-cost workshops in local computer stores and at civic organizations. During these workshops they asked that anyone interested in more information about using a computer in their business fill out an information card. They then personally called each person who filled out a card, answered their questions and determined if they were prospective customers. If so, they set up a personal appointment to close the sale.

Since it sometimes takes at least 20 calls to make a sale, the key to telephone sales or any form of sales is to keep making contacts. You can figure that every "no" you hear brings you that much closer to a "yes."

Although you will need basic selling skills, you may not want to sell your product or service yourself.

CHAPTER 34

USEFUL MIDDLEMEN?

Retail stores

You can sell your products through retail stores, either on consignment or with an open account. Consignment selling is where you leave your products with the retailer and if they sell, the retailer pays you typically 50% to 70% of the selling price. With an open account, the retailer should pay you at the end of some reasonable period of time, whether the products have sold or not.

To get shelf space for your products in retail stores you'll need to sell the owner of the store or buyer on your product. You'll need to spend a considerable amount of time in following up on getting payment, stocking and maintaining personal contact with the store. Retail stores usually do not pick up a single product. They are more likely to be interested in a line of products.

Wholesalers, agents, brokers and reps

Wholesalers are middlemen who buy from you and then they sell to the retail stores. Wholesalers buy for a demand that already exists, so you probably will not be able to locate a wholesaler until your product is already selling well.

You can get business, however, through agents, brokers and manufacturer's reps. These commissioned salespersons act as middlemen between you and buyers. The rapid growth of the off-the-shelf software market, for example, has created the software broker. The software broker acts as an agent between you and software publishers, manufacturers or end users.

Directories and listing services

Somewhat similar to this are directories and listing services. You will pay to be listed in directories that are distributed to your potential buyers. One such directory for example is *Leading Consultants in Computer Software & Programming* which lists over 5,000 independent programmers.

The book *Programmer's Market*, published by Writer's Digest Books, lists software publishers and arcade game manufacturers who will publish software produced by freelance programmers or will contract with freelance programmers.

SECTION 6

WORKING WITH WORDS

CHAPTER 35

WHY AUTOMATE?

As a general rule, automation makes repetitive tasks easy and time effective. Of course, there is always a learning curve — setting up a new system takes time and effort. But once the system is set up, routine, repetitive tasks become much more manageable. After the initial investment in time, a word processing program pays large dividends. Besides time, there is another consideration for the home based business: image.

Using a word processing program, most small businesses can create a very professional image. A relatively minor investment in equipment and programs allows the small business to look as professional as one of the big boys. A word processing program lets you type material in, revise it, check spelling, and format — or lay out — your letter or other written material before you commit it to paper. Using printers and typefaces with a little care and cleverness, any business can present a top quality image.

Consider one major task for every home based business — marketing. Most word processing programs allow you to send out the same letter to a large list of people — all in record time. With the feature called mail merge you can enter all of your addresses into the computer, like you would in your rolodex. Then type a letter, add a few codes where names are to go and the computer and printer will print all the letters, inserting individual names and addresses in the proper places on your letter and your envelope. You can even make mailing labels from the same "rolodex" file.

Marketing letters are one example of the way that automating with a word processing program will save time.

Other advantages to automating

Let's elaborate on some other possible advantages a word processing program has for your home business. These are just some of the time saving and image boosting features available to you with most word processing software:

Reference materials on screen

How would you like a dictionary, spell checker and thesaurus all at your fingertips? Most word processing programs make these available to you for instant use. They stay hidden and can be brought to the screen by pressing one or two keys without losing or leaving the project you are working on. Just think of the time saved by not having to thumb through pages of thick, heavy books. The program does the work for you. That little jog from the machine can help you vary and improve your use of the English language.

Standardizing repetitive work

Do you have a form you use over and over? You can generate a "template," or blank copy of this form every time you need it. Call up the template, fill in the blanks, and print! Invoices are one such use. Create a standard invoice form, pull the name and address from your on-line "rolodex" and let the program give you the next invoice numbers in your series. You've made a good start. But the descriptions of goods or services can also be standardized. You can create files of standardized or "boiler plate" text to enter into invoices. Inside the invoice form, you can pull up a boiler plate description. If the description needs modification for a particular job, you can modify it without changing the boiler plate text. Save the invoice copy for yourself, print, and go on to the next task.

Table of contents and indexes

Many larger documents are easier to read and use if you add a Table of Contents or an Index. Most word processing programs will let you mark your Table of Contents and Index entries in your document. You can then automatically generate a Table of Contents and an Index. This is another valuable time saver when you create a document. But, better yet is that when you revise the document, the Table of Contents and Index can be re-generated to automatically reflect the new page locations, if any, since you set it up before the revisions!

Mathematical calculations

Do you generate letters or other documents that require mathematical calculations? Most word processing programs have built in calculators which are instantaneously available. This comes in pretty handy for totalling those invoices, or columns of numbers that may be included in your document.

Spreadsheet linking

Do you already use a spreadsheet program for some of the work of your business? If you do, you probably need to incorporate numbers from the spreadsheet in text documents from time to time. Most word processing programs will allow what is called spreadsheet linking. This feature allows you to merge information from your spreadsheet file into your text file. You don't need to retype any of the numbers from the spreadsheet into your document.

Graphs and charts

If you use graphs and charts to present ideas or information to clients or prospective clients, most word processing programs will let you merge graphic files from other programs into your text file.This can make for a much more attractive final document.

Using lists

How many lists do you use in your business — besides that rolodex? You can create a list of sources, a list of clients, a list of parts, a list of part numbers, a list of projects, anything you might need. And once that list is entered, in any order, most programs let you sort your lists alphabetically or numerically in ascending or descending order. You can keep simple data in an easily accessible format and put it in the order you need at any given time.

Typefaces

Do you need different styles of type available for your text? Are you tired of running down to the local typesetter? Most computers allow you to use many different typefaces and styles in your word processing program. These are easily changed within your text document, and it adds to that professional look.

CHAPTER 36

IT'S EASY TO CONVERT

Scanning words

Optical Character Recognition (OCR) scanners read typed text and convert it into a file your computer can use. These have become very sophisticated, and can read almost any size print and store the document automatically on your computer disk. Be warned, you will probably have to edit the text. You should always plan to carefully read and check the new document, but the time saved from having to re-type all your documents into files on the computer is fantastic.

OCR scanners range from very simple, inexpensive systems, to ones which cost thousands of dollars and convert nearly any text to a computer file.

Pictures too?

Scanners can also convert pictures or images on a page to a computer file you can store for future use. Once scanned, images stored on disk can be edited and inserted into documents. In addition, you can often improve the quality of the picture you print out. Image scanners require special software and make demands on your printer. Check out image scanners requirements to be sure you have the equipment necessary to use the it effectively.

Choosing a scanner

Different scanners have different features and are best for different jobs. Some scanners can only "read" black and white line drawings while others can scan sophisticated halftone photos at up to 256 grey levels. Some can even scan color photographs. Most scanners can be used to "read" type, but you will need special OCR software to do the conversion to a text file. The scanner will only read the type as a picture which you will not be able to edit. The OCR software will convert it to text which you can use in the same way as text entered from the keyboard. Better OCR software will even allow you to preserve all of the fancy formatting in the original.

Be sure you buy what will best serve your needs. Make sure the software you pick and the scanner you choose work well together. Many scanners come bundled with software that is compatible. No matter what you pick, be sure you also have the cables or other accessories you will need. Also make sure that you will physically be able to hook the scanner up to your computer, that is, which "slot" or"port" you will need to use. Is that slot or port available on your computer or are you using it for something else?

Getting a service bureau to scan your documents

If your budget will not allow the cost of a scanner, you might want to use a service bureau to have your document(s)/image(s) scanned and transferred to a computer file for you. You can find a service bureau listed under computer services in the telephone directory. If you don't see one, try calling a print shop and ask them to refer you to someone, or call a type-setting service — who might be able to help you or refer you to someone who can.

Be clear about what you want from the service bureau and get an explanation of prices and what services are covered ahead of time. Quite often,the service bureau will ask you to bring in samples of the material you might want converted and will only make a quote at that time. Some service bureaus will also test one or two pages of material to assure themselves they will be able to work with your documents.

To determine if they can help you, the service bureau will also need to know what type of word processing software you are using and what kind of computer you work on. For your own protection, be sure that the disks you receive are guaranteed to work in your computer.

CHAPTER 37

CHOOSING THE SOFTWARE THAT'S RIGHT FOR YOU

Before buying software you must take a careful look at your needs and your budget. There are a wide range of programs available and you should be able to pick the features you want at a cost you can afford. Some programs allow you to get started with a basic program and add on specialized features at a later date. If you already use a spreadsheet or database program, pick a word processing program that will easily work with what you already have.

One rule of thumb: friends are likely to insist you pick the program they use. If you ask a friend or colleague which program to buy, unless they hate their program, they are going to recommend it. No matter how initially confusing or frustrating the program, once they became comfortable with it, they become attached to it.

When I first thought of a word processing program, I thought about a product that would just help me speed up correspondence and improve the look of my proposal forms. But I found this was not the case at all. These so-called word processing programs did much more. The programs were more integrated and contained many helpful features that were a definite plus to productivity. Over the years, I have used many programs and found that all of them have good features and strong points.

CHAPTER 38

GETTING STARTED
THE NITTY GRITTY

Installing software is such an individual situation that we can't cover it here. However, you should note that many small computer stores will install software for you if you bring the computer in, or may, for a fee, come to your house. However, installation is normally so simple, if you allow time to read instructions carefully, you won't need any help. Be sure to get clear instructions on how to "configure" or adapt your word processing program for the printer and other peripherals that you will use with the package.

Many packages have a tutorial that will guide you through the process, teaching you how to use the many features of the program. There are also a number of books written to assist learning various software packages. Spend some time in your computer bookstore to find the material that makes the most sense to you.

First projects

Most people buy a package because they have an immediate need. And they only read the instructions or the parts of the instructions that solve the immediate problem. You may want to start out right away writing letters. You can get started with most word processing programs if you know how to: get into the program; navigate on the screen; enter words; edit or change what you have entered; save the letter you have written; and print your letter out.

When you first look at a program, find out how to get back into a file that you have saved. One suggestion: use lots of little files to save letters and documents. If your program permits flexibility in naming files, decide for yourself how you will distinguish between letters, proposals, envelopes, lists, and other documents and then use those rules every time you save your work. In the beginning, it is very easy to remember what you've done. Three months down the road you may not be able to find a letter if all your correspondence is named the same.

Another suggestion: despite a public sense that computers create a "paperless" office, you will still want to print out a file copy of every letter, proposal, list, and other document, both for your protection if files are lost or damaged and for ease in finding materials when you need them.

Basic editing

When composing your letter or correspondence you have all types of keyboard options available to you. You may notice keys like -> | (Tab Key), Ins (Insert), Del (Delete), <- Backspace (Backspace Key), PgUp(Page Up Key), PgDn (Page Down Key), and keys that have arrows facing north, east, south, and west (cursor navigation keys). With these keys you can create any document very easily. How does each one perform its job? Let's take some time to cover the basic function of each key and how it will help you in composing and working with your documents:

-> | (Tab Key)

This key allows you to indent your text. Most word processing software programs have what is called a ruler bar across the top of your screen with obvious marks evenly spaced across the top. Sometimes you will have to tell your program to display the ruler bar. The marks represent tab stop guides and will show you where your text will indent to when the -> | (Tab Key) is pressed. These stops also help when you need to align text or numbers in columns for tables.

Ins (Insert Key)

This key inserts additional text into your existing document. It works as a toggle for switching from insert mode to overtype mode. When you compose your document, you will notice a little marker which moves as you type. This is called your cursor. To insert text you would simply move the cursor key to the spot you want the text to appear, toggle on the insert key, and type in the additional information. (Some programs have different keys assigned for insert mode, but most word processing programs support the Ins key. Some programs do not even need an Ins key and will allow you to insert type wherever you move the cursor.)

Del (Delete Key)

This key deletes text to the right of the cursor on some systems and to the left on others.

<- Backspace (Backspace Key)

This key deletes text to the left of the cursor on some systems. Some programs assign this key to move the cursor to the left only without affecting your text.

PgUp (Page Up Key)

This key moves your cursor up to the top of your document window or document. Pressing this key initiates an automatic scroll upwards.

PgDn (Page Down Key)

As it sounds, this key is the opposite of the previous one and moves your cursor to the bottom of your document screen or document. Between the PgUp key and this key you can move up and down through your document at will.

Arrow Keys

These keys look like little arrows facing north, east, south and west. These keys move your cursor in the direction of the arrow key selected. To move the cursor up one line you would use the up arrow key. The cursor would then jump up to the previous line in the exact position it occupied when underneath.

These keys allow you to get around your document much more easily than the page keys and make creating and editing your documents very easy. You can also use a mouse to replace your use of the keys in many instances. Using the mouse makes highlighting text and certain other functions lightning fast.

Some word processing programs also integrate more complex features. With the mouse, scrolling through your document can be instantaneous. The mouse replaces some keystrokes you would otherwise type to perform a function

(The mouse can do other things as well, such as selecting files to open. Rather than typing the filename, you can just place the mouse cursor on the filename and "click" the mouse button. The file will immediately load. You didn't

even have to remember the name much less
type it!)

CHAPTER 39

BASIC WORD PROCESSING

Search and replace

This feature describes exactly what it does. You can find a character or strings of text, and then have the option of replacing it with another string of text. This feature can be used to find every instance of what you are looking for. You don't have to sit and read your document to find them.

If you had just spent two years writing a novel and a publisher says, "I'd love to buy it but there's one problem with that character Monique. That name just doesn't fit. Change it to

Monica and I'll advance you $50,000." Well, there you are with 500 pages of prose to change before you can sign a contract. Doing this manually would be very time consuming and no fun at all. However, by using this global search and replace, your word processing software would take care of this for you. You would just tell it to replace the word "Monique" with the word "Monica" every time it appeared.

Most word processing programs will either automatically globally replace every instance a string of text appears or show you every one and allow you to decide. The latter can be a lot safer. Let's say you want to replace the word "to" with "from" in your document. If you did not specify to search for " to" with spaces around it and picked the global replace option, or you did not tell it to accept only instances where it was the entire word, the word "from" would appear in every word where the "to" string occurred. So the word that read "in*to*" would then read "in*from*." This feature is very powerful, so use it wisely. Drink your coffee while you babysit the task.

Block move or cut and paste

This is another very handy feature. Let's say you wanted to swap two paragraphs in your document. In other words, move one paragraph below or above the other. You would simply mark the text you wanted to move, according to your word processing software instructions, move the cursor to where you wanted to insert this marked text and perform the block move function according to your software instructions. Voila! The text is moved.

Some software will require you to select the block of type to be moved, cut it and paste it wherever you indicate it is to be inserted. You can even copy a block or string of type, or a letter, and paste it in another spot. Then you'll have it twice in the document!

This saves you from having to retype the information in the area you decided you wanted it.

Thesaurus

Let's say you're still writing that novel. You write your sentence, but want a word with more impact. Most word processing programs will allow you to automatically call up an online Thesaurus. Usually, you will highlight the word you want to check on, and initiate the Thesaurus. Your screen would automatically show all words which relate to the highlighted word in your document. You would then simply select the new word and the word processing program would automatically replace the highlighted word with the new selected word.

Spell Checker

Your document is completed and you want a quick and dirty method of checking your spelling. Most word processing programs have built in spell checking programs which contain standard dictionaries. The spell check program will check your document and prompt you whenever it finds a word it does not recognize. Some spell checkers will give you a list of of suggested spellings which you can select from. Others simply prompt you to manually fix the questionable word.

One word of warning: you should never rely on a spell check program to create a final document. You must always proof your document after running a spell check. There are still instances a spell check program cannot recognize (for example, the word "to" as opposed to the word "too"). Spell checkers are not perfect. Sometimes they will suggest replacing a perfectly good word with a word that doesn't make one bit of sense. But they're still worth running as they will spot mistakes you may miss.

CHAPTER 40

ADVANCED
WORD PROCESSING

Basic tools aid you in preparing a document with a minimum of time and effort. You may be very pleased just to have these tools, but the help doesn't stop there. There are other very handy features which can make life very easy using your computer.

Mail merge

Mail merge performs a myriad of functions. Why is it called Mail Merge? Well, from a basic "rolodex" type of input file you can insert names, addresses, phone numbers and whatever else into documents. You can also use this same list for generating envelopes and mailing labels. This is very handy when the same letter has to be mailed to many different individuals.

Text merge

Text Merge is invaluable when the same text must be used over and over in multiple documents. A perfect example is a law office. There may be standard clauses concerning documents generated. You can simply mark in your document where you want these pre-existing clauses included, and call up the file. The text is instantaneously entered where selected.

Block save

Block save is the opposite of text merge. Let's say you have a master contract and want to save chunks of it to boiler plate files. You can simply block (mark) the selected text and save it to a separate disk file. Use these smaller files to build larger, custom documents.

Page numbering

Page numbering allows you to specify where you want page numbers entered in your document (i.e. left bottom, right bottom, center, etc.). You can also specify the page number character format (i.e. 1, i or I). Once this is selected, your document will automatically be numbered for you.

You can also tell the word processing program to start numbering pages at a certain number other than one. Use this option when you have one document broken up into separate files. When you find out where the page number of the first file ends, you can then open the second file and specify to begin numbering at that point.

Text Alignment/Columns

Text and column alignment allows you to create a custom look for your document. For example, you may want certain text in your document to stand out a certain way. Maybe you want your text to appear in two or three columns.

You may want all of your text to align evenly along the right and left margins. This is called justification. All text will line up flush left and right. Or you may want your text to only line up on the left, or the right, and be ragged on the other side.

Headers and footers

Let's say you want the same thing typed in the same way in the same place on every page of the document you are working on. If you wanted this on the top of every page, you would be creating a header. If you wanted this on the bottom of every page, you would be creating a footer. Your word processing software will permit you to select and enter this information. Also, you can enter your page numbering in headers and footers to create a more uniform look to your document.

Split screen

Have you ever been working on something and needed to reference another document? With the split screen feature you can invoke a command to split your screen vertically or horizontally. You can then load documents you want to look up in the empty part of your split screen. This comes in very handy to check boiler plate text, or to use the block move feature mentioned earlier.

Some computer systems will have you make your window smaller and open a second window for a document just as you had the first one.

Word count

If you write long documents, such as articles, books, or term papers, you may want a particular number of words. Most word processing software programs have a feature that will count the number of words in your document. Some will also count characters or paragraphs or even lines. This eliminates manual counting or "guestimating", and gives you an exact number of words actually used.

Macros.

You can set up what is called a macro which stores your keystrokes for repetitive actions. These "recorded" activities can be typed into a document by invoking one command. One common use is to standardize an interoffice memo. You would initiate the macro feature and type in all the repetitive data such as TO:, FROM:, DATE:, and SUBJECT:. Once all the common data is entered, then you would save the sequence of keystrokes and assign a "hot key" which would invoke that macro when needed in the future. This may sound a bit complex, but once you try it you may feel like a magician when you see it work.

Revision marking

If you perform many edits on your documents, this feature will "strike out" text that is eliminated so you can refer to it when proofing your document. A more common term is called "redlining."

Automatic line numbering

Most word processing programs will allow you to automatically insert numbers before lines typed on a page. An obvious use for this is in law offices where many legal documents have the text line numbered. This makes referring to text and pages very easy. This is also very helpful since you don't have to line up pages in your printer to match preprinted lined paper.

Forms design

If you generate invoices, or use any type of form in your business, most word processing programs will allow you to set up a "template." When the form "template" is called up onto your screen, you will not have to type in the repetitive information, and the cursor will automatically skip to the spaces where text needs to be filled in. Some form"templates" will also allow you to "import" information from your "rolodex" file, and allow you to perform calculations if needed.

Sorting text

Do you ever need to make lists of things in your documents and then sort them? Let's assume you just want to enter the data and not have to figure anything out before inputting it. Most word processing programs have a sorting feature which will automatically sort the information for you in ascending or descending order either by number or alphabetically.

Using graphics from other software programs

Do you need to generate documents which include a graph or chart from a spreadsheet, a presentation chart, or an art program? Most word processing programs now have the capability to insert pre-existing graphics files from other programs.

Desktop publishing capabilities

Most word processing programs are getting very sophisticated in what is called Desktop Publishing. Aside from being able to use spreadsheet, database or graphics files, you can also add a very professional look to your documents. Most word processing programs now come with or allow multiple typefaces;, the ability to add lines, boxes and borders, and a view mode to see what the final document is going to look like.

These are some of features previously included only with popular desktop publishing programs.

Why choose a desktop publishing program over a fully integrated word processing program?

True desktop publishing programs have many features word processing programs lack. The items mentioned above are usually enough for the average person, but there are some very strong advantages to using a desktop publishing program. Although most word processing programs incorporate the feature we are about to mention, all desktop publishing programs have what is called a WYSIWIG (**What You See Is What You Get**) display. This eliminates using the view mode as you can actually see your project progress as it is happening. This saves a tremendous amount of time.

Additionally, desktop publishing programs contain many additional sophisticated typographical commands. This allows these programs to grow with you. They support (can read) many many more software programs than the word processing programs do. These programs also support many popular word processing programs because they are not useful for word processing although they do include that ability. They are unmatched for creating sophisticated, complex final pages, though.

CHAPTER 41

A FINAL NOTE
ON WORKING WITH WORDS

Do your homework when buying equipment or software. A bargain computer or printer may not be as compatible as you hope. It pays to talk to friends and read computer magazine reviews. Otherwise you may make a big mistake. Buy the best you can afford with the features you need, and do not waste money on bells and whistles you do not need, unless you may need them later. Money saved on buying hardware and software is often not a bargain. You pay for it in lower quality work and more time spent in preparing it. The quality of your work and your time are your biggest assets in any business. This is especially true when selecting printers, because the next version of your software program may not support it!

Also, when purchasing your software, find out what other popular word program files it will read or write to. Again, this will help make your business more versatile and open it up to many more customers.

SECTION 7

WORKING WITH NUMBERS

CHAPTER 42

DO I NEED TO COMPUTERIZE MY ACCOUNTING?

The first thing you must determine is whether you really need to keep your books on your computer. This may sound like a strange question to ask in a book about using computers in your business, but its importance cannot be stressed enough.

Many people have tried to use computing power where it is inappropriate. Accounting is

---

one place where you may not need to use your computer.

Checkbook accounting

Many small businesses find that they can make do with just a checkbook in which they record cash transactions. This system is simple. Record deposits and the source of those deposits and add the amount to the previous balance. Record checks written and who they were made payable to and subtract the amount from the previous balance. Most of you have done this for most of your business and personal lives without thinking about it. This system will only tell you how much you have available to spend at any given point in time. What it does not tell you is whether you are earning a profit, breaking even or spending more than you take in. When this kind of information is important, then a simple checkbook will not tell you everything you need to know to run your business effectively.

You won't know whether that word processing job you did for that law firm was profitable. You won't know if you lost money on a particular job because you quoted a rate that was below what it actually cost you to do it. You won't have the feedback needed to provide intelligent estimates to prospective customers in the future. Thus, by itself, the checkbook only gives limited information of limited value.

A cash basis

Most businesses get around the problem by expanding the checkbook by adding additional columns to allow analysis to be made of where the cash came from and what it was spent on. This will now allow some measure of profitability. It is still of limited usefulness since you can only measure what came in and what went out. Profitability is determined by comparing the two figures. If more came in than went out, you might think you earned a profit. If more went out than came in, you might think you lost money. If the two amounts were the same, you might say that you broke even. This is overly simplistic and may not reflect what happened during the period. The following example will illustrate this point.

Gerald Micawber earned $2,000.00 providing word processing services to a local law firm. During the month he spent $2,500.00 for a new laser printer to replace the dot matrix printer he had used for the last two years. Gerald had no other income and did not buy anything else that month. Gerald was unhappy because he felt that he had lost $500.00 that month. Did he really lose $500.00 that month? No!

Gerald overlooked the fact that this printer would make him more productive and provide better looking output for his clients in future time periods. Thus, by buying the new laser printer, Micawber had invested in making his product better and more useful to his customers.

This illustrates what accountants call the cash basis of accounting. It also illustrates where some of the problems with this method lie.

How many transactions?

One of the signs that indicate that you need to use a computer for accounting purposes is provided by the number of cash transactions that you must record during a particular time period. The larger the number of these transactions, the greater your need to automate the recording. If these transactions are also complex, then automating the recording process will make your life easier.

How do you tell if your transactions are complex? Let us consider the purchase of a superburger special at the local fast food restaurant as an example of an outwardly simple transaction that really is complex.

Mary Jones orders a superburger special at her local Jiffy Burger. All Mary sees is the clerk push two buttons on the register: one for the product and one for the quantity. The register rings up the price including sales tax while the clerk picks up a finished superburger special from the appropriate bin. The cash register is actually a point-of-sale terminal that not only records the appropriate amount of cash received from Mary but also updates inventory to reflect that two quarter pound beef patties, one hamburger bun and the various other items included in the superburger special have been taken out of inventory. This information will be used at some point in time to measure the quantities of these materials used in addition to the quantity of superburger specials sold. It will also determine when a new order for replacement patties, buns and other items is placed. Thus, the simple transaction of buying a hamburger for lunch is not really so simple. This detail would be impossible without a computer.

Your business will probably not sell hamburgers, but the principles illustrated may apply to your business anyhow. If you must keep track of many items that go into your product or service, you will want to use your computer to do it. This will reduce the chance for error and allow you to spend more time doing business rather than recording what you have done.

CHAPTER 43

HOW MUCH
DO I NEED TO KNOW?

I would like to tell you that you don't need to know any accounting or bookkeeping to keep accounting records on a computer. I can't do this because you need some knowledge to design your accounting system and set up the correct procedures to keep it working correctly. If you don't know anything about this subject, all is not lost. All you have to do is get the right help. This help can be obtained by hiring a bookkeeper or a bookkeeping service or an accountant. If you want to learn some accounting you can take a course at your local college.

These courses will give you a good understanding of the procedures which accountants and bookkeepers follow. It will not make you either an accountant or bookkeeper. You will learn the rudiments of accounting but not how to design an accounting system to meet the needs of your business. To further complicate the issue, these courses are not taught with the idea that this is all you will ever need to know about accounting since the accounting field is too broad to be covered in a one or two semester sequence. It certainly won't hurt you to do this and it also may prove useful in running your accounting system.

Outside help is available

There are many bookkeeping services that will keep track of your accounting information and produce your monthly reports for you. These range from people who will do the work on your equipment at your convenience to those that merely pick up your checkbook information each month and process the information in accordance with your requests. Some of these businesses are homebased; others are not. Some of the individuals running these services are very knowledgeable in all phases of accounting and with various industries. If you choose this approach, look for someone who knows your particular kind of business since that will make system design easier for both of you.

You may also seek the help of a CPA. CPAs are licensed accountants who may or may not be familiar with your industry or the problems faced by homebased businesses. Never choose an accounting firm that is much bigger than you are since you will be paying for services you either do not need or cannot adequately use. Certified Public Accountants are generally thought to be experts about all tax and accounting matters for every individual or business. This isn't true. Many CPAs specialize in particular industries or areas of accounting. Try to find one who knows homebased businesses, your industry and is computer knowledgeable. This sounds easier than it is since there are few CPAs in practice who can combine all three.

You will also want to find a CPA that you feel comfortable with. His bedside manner may often prove as important as any other factor in a satisfactory long-term working relationship.

CHAPTER 44

CHOOSING A SYSTEM

Another influence on the design of an accounting system is the kind of business in
which you are engaged. If you are in a service
business, you will have to keep track of time
spent and materials used for billing purposes.
If you are in a manufacturing business, you will
have to keep track of inventories of raw materials, work-in-process (unfinished items) and finished goods ready for sale. If you are in a
wholesale or retail industry, you will have to
keep track of accounts receivable and accounts
payable. If you have employees, you will have

to maintain payroll records. Each of these will exert a strong influence on what your accounting system must do and what you must know to operate it correctly and reliably.

What hardware do I need?

A common error most people make is to buy computer equipment before determining what software they need or want to run on it. This is not a fatal error but can result in either buying too much equipment or not enough. If you already have your computer, you must find out if it can run the software you need. If it can't, you will either have to upgrade it or replace it.

Most of the low end accounting software on the market can run on a 640K RAM PC with either two high density floppy disk drives or one high density floppy and a 10 megabyte hard disk. A Mac Plus with a hard drive and two meg of internal memory is the minimum Macintosh equipment you will be able to use. It is not necessary to have color graphics but it is useful.

An ideal configuration is a 640K RAM PC-AT compatible (80286 microprocessor) with an 80387 math coprocessor, one high density floppy disk drive, a 20 or 40 megabyte hard disk, VGA graphics and monitor, and a good wide carriage dot matrix printer. This configuration should cost between $2,000.00 and $2,500.00 depending on the brand of machine you get.

If you have a two disk 8088 microprocessor based PC (IBM PC or PC-XT compatible) you may find that you cannot get the most out of the available accounting software. In this case, you should at least upgrade to a 10 megabyte hard disk and obtain an 8087 math coprocessor.

Why do you need the math coprocessor? This chip will speed up all calculations, thus allowing you to process more information in the same amount of time. Speed is especially important with complex accounting packages on 8088-based computers since you can actually wait 15 to 20 minutes to process certain information without the math coprocessor.

What accounting software should I buy?

This is a tough question to answer. You should buy the software you are able to handle and that meets your needs. I have seen many cases of people buying a $49.95 accounting software package with the idea that they will be able to save all those fees they paid to their accountant only to discover that they could not use the software because they did not have the knowledge to run and install it. This usually resulted either in abandonment of the software or in the hiring of a consultant to install and set up the procedures and controls required to run the systems. Don't expect to say goodbye to your accountant or expect to get a bargain unless you know enough to do the work yourself.

The accounting software to buy will be determined by what you need to do and how you need to do it.

Factors to consider

Type of Organization:
Corporation
Partnership
Sole Proprietorship.
Basis of Accounting:
Cash
Accrual or Tax
Industry:
Service
Wholesale/Retail/Mail Order
Manufacturing

Type of organization

The sole proprietorship is the easiest form of business organization since it only requires that an individual decide to go into business, obtain the necessary licenses (if required), open a bank account, obtain insurance and announce that you are in a particular line of business to start a business. This type of organization will also require the simplest accounting system since all transactions will result in either increasing or decreasing the owner's investment in the business.

Partnerships are almost as easy to form as sole proprietorships except that two or more people must agree to open a business. They must still obtain the proper licenses, open a bank account, obtain insurance and announce that they are in business.

Accounting for a partnership is more complicated than a sole proprietorship since income and losses must be allocated to each of the partners by some prearranged formula or by the method described in the Uniform Partnership Act.

The corporation is a completely different kind of organization since it is recognized as being an individual by law. That means that a corporation has a life separate and distinct from its owners who are called stockholders. There are two kinds of corporations in existence today: The Subchapter S Corporation and the Subchapter C Corporation. The sole difference between the two is how they are taxed. The Subchapter S corporation is taxed as a partnership with each stockholder paying income tax on his or her proportionate share of the corporation's income. The Subchapter C Corporation pays its own taxes on income. If the remaining income is then distributed to the stockholders (called dividends), they pay tax on the amount of dividends received. Thus, the earnings of a C Corporation may be subject to double taxation. Accounting for the stockholders investment and accumulated profits is again different from that for a partnership or sole proprietorship. It makes no difference whether you are an S Corporation or C Corporation at least as far as the accounting system is concerned.

Basis of accounting

Each form of organization has a recommended (and sometimes a required) basis of accounting.

The cash basis of accounting described in an earlier example is based upon the theory that recognition and recording of revenue does not occur until payment is received from the customer and expenses are not recognized and recorded until paid to the vendor. The shortcoming of this method is that it ignores the possibility that some expenditures may benefit more than one specific period as illustrated in the Micawber example. This basis of accounting is usually used in service businesses since the method parallels the way these firms operate.

Accrual basis accounting is different. Under this basis, revenues are recognized and recorded when earned rather than when payment is received. Expenses are recognized and recorded when incurred and not when paid.

Imagine John Doe runs a court reporting and word processing service catering to the needs of law firms. He has taken a deposition from Mary Stewart who is a client of the law firm of Takim, Boxim and Beatim. John types up the deposition and sends it and a bill for $100.00 to the law firm on November 14. He receives payment for his services on December 5.

Under the cash basis of accounting, John would not have any income until December 5 when he receives payment from Takim, Boxim and Beatim. Under the accrual basis of accounting, John would recognize and record income of $100.00 on November 14 since he had completed the job on that date. Takim, Boxim and Beatim would not recognize any expense until they paid the bill on December 5 under the cash basis. Under accrual basis accounting, they would recognize and record an expense of $100 on November 14 because John has completed the work assigned to him on this date.

The accrual basis of accounting has one advantage over cash basis accounting. It recognizes that some expenditures may provide benefits to the firm in more than one accounting period. An example of such an expenditure is the $1,500.00 Mr. Micawber paid for the new laser in our earlier example. The laser printer is useful in many accounting periods and not just the one in which it was bought. In effect, the expenditure has given Micawber the ability to provide better service to his customers.

There is a third basis of accounting that has seen some acceptance in recent years. That basis is called the income tax basis of accounting. Under this method, the books are kept in accordance with the income tax rules in effect at the time. The major difficulty with this method is that income tax rules have changed on the average of every nine months since the mid-1950s. To further exacerbate the problem the rules sometimes are not defined until several years after the tax laws are passed.

It is not uncommon to find that companies use hybrid accounting having elements of two or even all three of cash, accrual and tax. One such example is the modified cash basis where revenues are not recognized and recorded until payment is received but expenses are recognized and recorded when incurred. This method is quite commonly found in small businesses where cash received is a good measure of income since the time between the completion of the work and the receipt of payment is very short.

Industry standards

Each particular industry has its own particular trade practices and requirements that must be reflected in your accounting system. These industry practices may be similar to those used in other businesses. Thus, retail merchants and professional services firms will probably recognize income when cash payment is received. On the other hand, the industry practices may be very different. Thus, a construction firm may bill for and receive progress payments while a particular project is being built and recognize these payments as income even though they haven't really completed the job.

Most of the low cost accounting packages will handle most of the accounting requirements you may have. Some of these packages do the job better than others for certain types of businesses so you must know what the capabilities of these packages are. How does one find out about what a particular package can do? Read reviews in the various computer and accounting magazines. Speak to other homebased businesses to see what they are using. Ask your accountant to recommend something for you.

Accounting software ranges in price from $50 to $7,500. The price does not suggest that the software is capable of doing more. The higher priced programs do have more features and are more flexible, but they are also more complex to operate. Do not select the software solely based on price since a cheap package may end up costing more in time and aggravation and you will have to live with the choice you make. I have found that it is better to pay a little more for software that offers a better promise to do what you need done.

(You will find a listing of most of the good accounting packages at the end of this chapter.)

CHAPTER 45

PREPARING YOURSELF FOR THE COMPUTER

Chart of accounts

The first thing you must do when installing your accounting software is to set up a chart of accounts. A chart of accounts is a listing of all the categories of items of which you wish to keep track. The chart of accounts is a table of contents of your general ledger. As mentioned earlier, you must know what you are doing at this stage or you will find that you will need to change it often.

Your chart of accounts will vary depending upon the kind of business you are in and the kind of organization you have selected. Most inexpensive accounting packages have built-in charts of accounts to make things a bit simpler, and many offer a selection of charts of accounts based on different industries. Remember that even these are general purpose and may or may not meet your needs.

All charts of accounts follow the basic accounting equations:

Assets = Liabilities + Owner(s)' Equity

Net Income = Revenues - Expenses
where expenses are less than revenues

Net Loss = Revenues -Expenses
where revenues are less than expenses

Owner(s)' Equity = Owner(s)' Investment + Net Income -Net Loss -Owner(s)' Withdrawals.

These equations form the basis for the basic financial statements you can obtain from the accounting system periodically.

Balance sheet

The first equation is called the balance sheet equation since it consists of the three elements found in this statement. Assets represent valuable economic resources, consisting of tangible or intangible property, from which future benefits can be obtained by its owner. Examples of assets are cash, accounts receivable, inventories, land, buildings, equipment, and automobiles. These items should be listed in accordance with how easily they can be converted into cash without resulting in the dissolution of the business. Thus, a car service would be out of business if it were to sell off its automobiles. A wholesaler could convert its receivables into cash and still remain in business.

Liabilities represent claims against the assets of a business by parties to whom the business owes money. These consist of accounts payable, taxes payable, payroll payable and the like. Also included would be mortgages on property owned or controlled by the business. This category has sometimes been called creditor(s)' equity since it can also be viewed as the investment made by this group in the business.

Owner(s)' Equity represents the investments made by the owner from the inception of the business plus the results of operating the business since that time less amounts taken out of the business by the owner either in the form of cash, merchandise or other assets. This is shown by the last equation.

Income statement

The middle two equations are really the same equation showing the expected results given the assumptions shown. They can be called the income statement equations since they reflect the effects of subtracting from the revenue earned by a business the costs of earning that revenue. Revenues can be defined as

income derived from operating the business.
Expenses are defined as the costs of producing
that revenue.

CHAPTER 46

CHART OF ACCOUNTS REDUX

The chart of accounts is divided into five sections: Assets; Liabilities; Owner(s)' Equity; Revenues; Expenses. The accounts defined within each of these groupings will vary based upon how your business is run and the kind of business you are in.

Merchandising businesses will have asset accounts called "Merchandise Inventory" that contain the value of the inventory determined at some point in time. They will have accounts called "Sales," "Sales Returns and Allowances," and "Sales Discounts" in the revenue section to record sales of merchandise, the return of merchandise, or price reductions of merchandise after they are sold. They will also have expense accounts called "Purchases," "Purchase Returns and Allowances," and "Purchase Discounts" to record the cost of the merchandise purchased for resale, merchandise returns, or price reductions of merchandise after purchase.

Manufacturing firms will have their inventory accounts in the assets section. These will be "Raw Materials," "Work-in-Process," and "Finished Goods." Raw materials represent what the product is made from. Work-in-Process represents those items that were started, but not completed at the end of an accounting period. Finished goods represent items completed but not sold at the end of a particular accounting period.

Service industries may have inventories, but the product sold consists primarily of the time the owner and his employees (if any) have available for performing services such as accounting, bookkeeping, marketing, consulting, writing, and so on, for customers. These cannot be inventoried because no dollar value can be assigned until they have been used.

Owner(s) equity

The Owner(s)' equity section of the chart of accounts will be determined by the form of organization of the firm. A sole proprietorship will have the following equity accounts:

John Doe, Capital
John Doe, Withdrawals.

The capital account is used to reflect investments made in the business by the owner since its inception. It is modified by the profits and losses of the business at the end of each accounting year. The withdrawals account is used to reflect the removal of cash or other assets from the business by the owner during the year. It is also offset against the capital account at the end of each accounting year. The purpose of setting up a separate account to handle withdrawals by the owner is to show the owner and the other users of the financial statements exactly how much he or she has taken out of the business at any given point in time during the year and at the end of the year.

The equity section of a partnership's chart of accounts is similar to that of a sole proprietorship in that there is a capital account and a withdrawal account for each partner as shown below for the partnership of Doe and Doe:

John Doe, Capital
John Doe, Withdrawals
Jane Doe, Capital
Jane Doe, Withdrawals

The capital accounts reflect the amounts invested by each particular partner since the inception of the partnership. Income and losses are allocated in accordance with some agreement or by statute if no agreement is in existence and added to or subtracted from each partner's capital account at the end of each accounting year. The withdrawal accounts serve the same purpose as that of a sole proprietor. The withdrawal accounts are offset against the individual partner's capital account at the end of each year.

A corporation's equity section looks different from the above because it is recognized as an entity separate and distinct from its owners by law. The owners are called stockholders and receive shares of stock in the business in exchange for their investments that can be in the form of cash or other assets.

The accounts are:

Capital Stock
Retained Earnings

Capital stock represents the value of the stock exchanged for the shares of stock issued to the investors. It is the amount invested by the original owners and does not necessarily reflect the current value of the stock held by the stockholders. Should a stockholder subsequently sell his or her interest to someone else, the capital stock account will remain unchanged regardless of whether the seller sold stock exchanged for the shares of stock issued to the investors. It is the amount invested by the original owners and does not necessarily reflect the current value of the stock held by the stockholders. Should a stockholder subsequently sell his or her interest to someone else, the capital stock account will remain unchanged regardless of whether the seller sold the stock at a gain or loss. Retained Earnings represent the total of accumulated profits and losses not paid out to stockholders since the inception of the business. These are kept separate from the capital stock since the corporation is under no legal obligation to pay anything to the stockholders. It can reinvest this money in the business, use it to acquire other companies, or simply allow it to accumulate interest in a bank account. The corporation may choose to pay dividends out of retained earnings in order to avoid an accumulated earnings tax. The stockholders may still have to pay income tax on the amount of dividends they receive.

CHAPTER 47

NUMBERING AND DEFINING ACCOUNTS

Numbering

Once you have decided upon your classifications, you should set up a rational numbering system for your accounts. These numbers will be used when entering transactions into the system to tell the computer how to classify and record the transactions. You might wonder why a number is used. It is simply because it is less time consuming to enter a number than it is to write out an account name. Thus, it is easier to say that cash received against an invoice sent to a customer should be applied against account

---

number 115 than to type in accounts receivable.

A good numbering system for a small or homebased business should not have more than five digits. Each place in the number should represent a different level of account. The first digit should identify the account category:

    10000 Asset
    20000 Liability
    30000 Owners Equity
    40000 Revenue
    50000 Expenses

The second digit may define a level within each category as follows:

    11000 Current Assets
    12000 Investments
    13000 Fixed Assets
    21000 Current Liabilities
    22000 Long term Liabilities
    51000 Cost of Merchandise
    52000 Manufacturing Expenses
    53000 Selling Expenses
    54000 General and Administrative Costs

The third and fourth digits can further define sub-categories, but the fifth or last digit must define an actual account with a dollar balance.

At this point you should be able to design your chart of accounts and the required numbering system. You should enter this into your accounting system at the appropriate point in its installation procedure.

Defining accounts

The next thing you will have to do is define certain accounts that will be used routinely. Most accounting software asks for the accounts to be used for:

Cash

In which bank account will checks normally be deposited?

Which bank account will checks be written on to pay accounts payable or payroll?

Accounts Receivable:

Which account will invoices to customers be accumulated in?

Inventories/Purchases:

Where to accumulate the cost of merchandise purchased for resale or raw materials purchased for use in a production process?

Accounts Payable:

Where to accumulate invoices received from vendors?

Payroll Taxes Payable:

Where to accumulate payroll taxes withheld from employee's paychecks?

Sales Taxes Payable:
Where to accumulate amounts collected for Sales Tax?

Sales:
Where to accumulate sales made on credit?

Payroll Expense:
Where to accumulate wages and salaries paid to employees?

Employer Paid Payroll Taxes:
Where to accumulate amounts paid by the employer on payroll.

This list is not meant to be exhaustive so there may be some questions not addressed. It should serve as a guideline to help you remember what information you must provide to the system.

CHAPTER 48

DEFINING STATEMENTS

The last step in the process is to define the financial statements that you will produce on a monthly, quarterly, or annual basis. This step simply consists of telling the computer which accounts should show up on which statement and how they should be combined on the statement.

There are three basic financial statements which all businesses should prepare periodically. These are Balance Sheet, Income Statement, and Statement of Cash Flows.

Balance Sheet

The Balance Sheet is a snapshot of the various balance sheet accounts at a particular point in time. The balance sheet accounts are those in the asset, liability and owners equity categories. These are accounts that always exist though the balances in them will change.

Income Statement

The Income Statement shows the results of operating the business over a particular period of time that is usually no longer than one year. The revenue and expense account balances are shown here. At the end of the year these accounts are zeroed out and the resulting net income or net loss amount is transferred to owners equity. These accounts are therefore considered to be temporary.

Statement of Cash Flow

The Statement of Cash Flows is not always necessary but can provide insight into where cash came from and what it was used for. This is a re-statement of the income statement and balance sheet from the point of view of how all the activities the firm engaged in effected its cash balance.

There are other industry specific financial statements you may wish to generate. Two of the most important are the Manufacturing Statement and the Job Cost Report.

Manufacturing Statement

The Manufacturing Statement reflects what was spent on producing the finished goods added to inventory during the year. In effect this provides the same information that purchases would in a merchandising business. The basic premise underlying this statement is that raw materials must be worked on in some way to produce a product that is ready for resale. These costs are added and the cost of the finished product is determined. The resulting amount, called the Cost of Goods Manufactured, is then shown on the Income Statement.

The Job Order Cost Report

The Job Order Cost Report shows the accumulated costs on a particular job. The purpose here is to measure how profitable a particular process was so that we can use this information in the future when bidding on similar contracts.

CHAPTER 49

FINAL STEPS TO
SETTING UP YOUR SYSTEM

At this stage, you are now almost ready to use your computerized accounting system. You may find that you need preprinted forms to do this. Check the manual that came with your accounting system to see where you can obtain these. Keep in mind that some publishers will offer their accounting product at a low price in order to encourage you to purchase the required forms from them. You will probably find that the forms they will sell you will cost more than similar forms sold by other companies.

There are many sources for forms to be used with accounting packages. These include places such as New England Business Systems (NEBS) and Nelco. Chances are you have already received a catalog in the mail from one of these firms. If not, look at a current computer magazine or Home Office Computing Magazine to find the location of the nearest forms supply house. You may also try your local stationery or computer store.

CHAPTER 50

USING YOUR BRAND NEW COMPUTERIZED ACCOUNTING SYSTEM

Your software is now installed. You've got your forms set up and loaded into your printer. You are now ready to begin using the accounting system.

The fun part of the process is finally here. You probably believe that all of your prayers have been answered. Don't fool yourself by believing that you have designed a foolproof system because you probably haven't.

I have designed many accounting systems and installed just about as many. I have yet to do one that was perfect the first time. This is caused by making decisions without enough information. You should realize that you will never get enough information until after the decision is made. All is not lost. Changes should and can be made without starting from scratch.

At this point you should test your system to see if works correctly. This is best done by feeding in information that should produce known results. Thus, I would test my billing module by actually making up a few test invoices to see if these print correctly and are properly recorded. Do not be afraid to make errors on purpose during this phase. It is not unusual to find that some of the accounting software will accept obviously incorrect information. On the other hand, some software will reject this. You should always be aware of this and test your system before you actually use it. You should also keep an eye open for obviously ridiculous results. You can spot them, often your computer cannot.

Once you are satisfied that the system is working correctly it is advisable to run it in parallel with the system you were using previously for some period of time. This will provide assurance that the system produces the information you were previously receiving. Significant differences do not necessarily mean that the new system is wrong. They should be investigated to determine if this is the case. If the system is producing incorrect information work backwards to see why and correct the problem.

Once you are satisfied that the new system works, drop the old system. This does not mean that the system is perfect yet. The fact that everything works correctly now does not mean that it will be that way forever. In fact, no accounting system can anticipate every possible transaction. You should find that 95% of your transactions are relatively routine. An additional 4% can easily be accommodated by your system. That last 1% will always be a problem whether you are computerized or not.

Please bear in mind that developing a computerized accounting system is not something that can be done in an hour or two. It requires time. Don't be discouraged because you are making little progress or because you have come to a seemingly insurmountable problem. Don't be afraid to ask questions. The key lies in asking the right person the question. That person can be a fellow homebased business person or your accountant.

Set up a schedule for entering data into the system. Make sure that you adhere to it. I often find that spending time at the beginning or end of the day recording information gives me some insight into what has happened previously. It also makes me think about what I have done right and what I have done wrong. There are valuable lessons to be learned in each situation. Doing this also allows me to keep things manageable by not allowing them to pile up.

RESOURCES

Accounting software falls into several categories based on their intended use.

Personal Managers

(useful for keeping track of personal financial resources and have some application to service oriented businesses)

For IBM Compatibles:

Money Counts, Parsons Technology, Cedar Rapids, IA,

Quicken, Intuit, Menlo Park, CA, (800)624-8742

For the Macintosh:

Quicken, Intuit, Menlo Park, CA, (800)624-8742

CheckFree, Columbus, OH. (800)882-5280

M.Y.O.B., Teleware, Parsippany, NJ, (800)322-6962

Low Cost Accounting Systems

(range in price from $99.95 to $995.00. It is in this category that most businesses will find what they need)

For IBM Compatibles:

Andrew Tobias Managaging Your Money, Westport, CT

DACEasy, Dallas, TX, (800)877-8088

Painless Accounting, Computer Software, Plano, TX, (214)596-9164

Computerized Classic Accounting, Absolute Solutions, Los Angeles, CA, (800)633-7666

Bedford and ACCPAC, Computer Assoc., San Jose, CA, (800)531-5236

PeachTree, Norcross, GA, (800)247-3224

One Write Plus, Great American Software, Amherst, NH, (800)528-5015

NewViews, Q.M. Page Assoc., Toronto, Ont., (416)923-4567

For the Macintosh:

Computerized Classic Accounting, Absolute Solutions, (800)633-7666

Multiledger, CheckMark Software, Ft. Collins, CO, (800)444-9922

AtOnee! and Insight Expert, Layered, Boston,MA, (800)622-4436

Andrew Tobias Managaging Your Money, Westport, CT

Moderate to High Cost Systems

(start at $1,000. They are extremely capable but require a knowledge of accounting to use effectively)

RealWorld, Concord, NH, (603)224-2200

Solomon, TLB, Findlay, OH, (419)424-0422

Great Plains, Fargo, ND, (800)345-3276

Platinum, Advanced Business Microsystems, Irvine, CA

MAS90, Sate of the Art, Costa Mesa, CA, (800)854-3056

AccountMate, SourceMate, Mill Valley, CA, (800)877-8896

Champion, Golden, CO, (800)243-2626

This list is not exhaustive. It is merely an indication of what is available on the market. As you can see, there is no dearth of computerized accounting systems ready to handle your business needs.

SECTION 8

SELLING YOURSELF

CHAPTER 51

YOUR MARKETING HAT

If you have a home-based business or plan on starting one, then one of the most important hats you wear is the one that says "Marketing and Sales Department." To succeed, you must be naturally good at it, or quickly develop the skill. Marketing and sales, if you strip away all the fancy terminology and mysticism, is simply determining which people are most likely to buy your product or service, where they can be found, telling them the benefits of your company and products or services, persuading them to buy from you, and getting them to buy again.

There's a major problem for you or any company trying to communicate with prospective customers—advertising "noise." Today, the typical consumer is bombarded by over 5,000 advertising messages a day. But even if your prospective customer receives your message, he might not remember it for long. Only one to three percent of all messages are remembered without prompting, according to a study commissioned by Whittle Communications. "Each year we send more [messages], and receive less," says Al Ries and Jack Trout in their classic book, *Positioning: The Battle for Your Mind* (Warner Books). They point out that "we have become the world's first over-communicated society."

So how can you get your message through? How can you compete with larger companies that spend much more on advertising and have dedicated staffs of marketing and sales professionals? First, you need to select and find only those prospects who will benefit *most* from your product or service. Second, you must make your message clearer and specifically directed at that small group of prospects, and third, you must repeat the message as many times as possible. Finally, once they're customers, you must have better and more personal service. A personal computer and specialized marketing and sales software can help you accomplish all of these functions.

For home businesses, there's never been a better time to use a computer to help you market and sell. The number and variety of sales and marketing software programs for personal computers has skyrocketed and many of them are reasonably priced. *Sales and Marketing Management Magazine* in their Annual Software Survey list several hundred programs for applications like account management, advertising, direct marketing, market analysis and research, sales management, and telemarketing.

Is it worth the effort to learn and apply marketing and sales software? Industry experts point out that sales people are 43% more productive with just a computer and the basic software packages, such as word processing. With specialized sales software, the average sales person can boost productivity by 80 to 300%. However, you just can't hand the computer a list of prospects and tell it to plan, create, and carry out the marketing and sales for you—at least not yet! It can't take your place as the company decision maker. A computer can help you organize, track, and follow up on prospects and customers, tell you what's working, and even train and advise you.

CHAPTER 52

LEARNING THE GAME

Is there a difference between marketing and selling? Unfortunately the words are used interchangeably. But they are different, albeit sometimes overlapping functions. Marketing and selling are part of a continuous process. The result of this process is clear, whether you use a computer or not. When you invest resources (time, effort, money) in marketing and sales, you build a "prospect bank account" that yields customers tomorrow, the next week, month and even a year later. So whether you spend a few hours a week, or hire someone to work full-time, you'll always need to market and sell as long as you're in business. "Even though the [sales and marketing] process is thought to be unstructured and unmeasurable, it's really quite simple to structure the work into several sub-processes," says Jack Caffey, Telesales and Customer Information Center Manager for Hewlett-Packard. A review of the steps of a marketing outline process can help you evaluate where and how a particular sales and marketing software package fits into the process.

The first step is an "Idea for a Product or Service." It might be for a totally new product or service, a modification of a current one, or even a new way to apply or market an old one.

Next comes "Market Research." It helps you determine the ideal prospects for your product or service and if there's enough of them around to start and support a business. You would also determine if the needs solved by your product or service are significant. The result of market research is a prospect profile that is used to select lists (data bases) of people to contact.

Before you contact your potential new customers, a "Marketing and Sales Plan" is developed to determine how you're going to communicate the benefits of your products and why prospects should buy from your company. Also, when someone does purchase your product or service, you need to consider how to turn them into repeat buyers.

Then you'll "Contact" your prospects. Prospects are contacted with marketing communication tools like ads, billboards, and press releases, or by sales people with in-person visits, phone calls, and letters. No matter how you find them, the results of your sales and marketing communication efforts are names of individuals who have shown some interest in your product or service. Some will be more interested than others, so you need to qualify them.

To "Qualify" prospects you question them, listen carefully to their answers, and look for nonverbal signs to understand how interested they are in your product or service. If you think they are likely to buy within a reasonable amount of time, they'll join a smaller list of qualified prospects. For professional sales people, these prospects become part of their monthly or quarterly "forecasted deals." You would then spend more time and effort trying to turn them into customers.

After qualifying the prospect, you need to "Sell" them your solution to their problem. Sell is a four-letter "swear" word to many people, but it's one of the keys to being a successful (home) business person. Sales doesn't mean fancy suits and pushy, manipulative behavior—everyone sells, you just might call it "turning on the charm" or something similar. It's your business, so it's up to you to convince the prospect that your product or service is the best solution for them. If you need help understanding the basics of sales thousands of books and courses on sales methods wait on the shelves, ready to teach you. Hopefully, the result of the selling step is an order.

The final step in the initial cycle is "Implementation." If you're selling a product, you might just ship or deliver it and then start the next step, turning them into repeat buyers. But some products like computer systems, and most services, are more complex. They often require on-going interaction, installation, and training before the customer is fully satisfied. At larger companies, it might take dozens of people to successfully implement and install the product or to provide the service.

When the customer is satisfied, it's much easier to get him to buy again. Repeat Sales or Account Growth, as HP's Caffey says, "is your opportunity to sell add-on and related products to enhance the customer's investment. Account growth is important because studies show that it costs five times as much to obtain a new customer as it does to sell additional product and services to a current one."

The common denominator in marketing and sales

The common denominator in marketing and selling, no matter what type of product or service, are the names of your prospects and customers. "The computer's ability to maintain a customer database— whatever the size of your company—is one of the most revolutionary marketing developments in a century. The computer which was once viewed as an impersonal threat that would regiment society has turned out to be the key to permitting companies to serve their customers far more personally than before," write Stan Rapp and Tom Collins in their book *MaxiMarketing* (Plume Books). A computer improves customer service by cutting the amount of time you spend administrating the marketing and sales process and making sure you follow-up before and after the sale.

Before you purchase any marketing and sales software, you first need to examine how you currently (or plan to) market and sell, and if you're already successful or not.

CHAPTER 53

YOUR COMPUTER
CAN HELP YOU SELL

If you're already successful in finding prospects and turning them into customers, then your interest in using a computer to market and sell might be to just automate some of the manual steps in the process. In this case, you'll use the software to help you track prospects and customers by documenting how you found them (phone call, referral, ad, direct mail), recording business and personal information, and reminding you when to contact them again. Knowing where each prospect and customer came from will give you an accurate picture of

---

what marketing activities work. You can then confidently invest more resources into those activities or compare new ones that you would like to try. The computer will also help you spend *less* time on marketing and sales administrative tasks like record keeping, which gives you more time to spend on activities that produce income. Remember, you only make money when you are actually *performing* the service or delivering the product, not when you're marketing, selling, or administrating.

Suppose, for example, that you run a successful office cleaning service that gets most of it's prospects from classified ads in local newspapers and phone books. With a computer you could track where they saw your ad, and some basic information like their name, address, phone number, square footage to clean, and how many times per month they want your service. Over the course of a year, you would then know what newspapers and phone books draw more prospects. You could also compare classified advertising with other marketing activities like handing out flyers or mailing discount coupons. When prospects respond to your ad, you can easily follow-up with a phone call or letter in a few days, week, or more. Regular follow-up is important since it often takes up to five contacts before a prospect will buy.

If you're not successful, or if you're starting a new business, you should start at the beginning of the sales and marketing process. You first need to research and plan.

CHAPTER 54

FINDING WHERE YOU WANT TO GO

Before you do any research or planning with a computer, it's a good idea to take a walk, or to find somewhere quiet and isolated, like a library, to brainstorm your product, company, and personal goals. A home business isn't an inflexible corporation,with policies and goals chiseled in stone and out of your control. Your goals are the goals of the company. So why spend all your time, energy, and resources going somewhere you don't enjoy? A clear, simple statement of your goals will help you focus your marketing efforts and always remind you of where you're going. Of course, your goals can change, but you'll have something written to review when a new opportunity or direction comes your way.

Market research

With firm goals in mind, you're ready to start gathering information on prospects, competitors, and industry. Today, the problem isn't finding information, it's trying to sort through it for something meaningful. You could spend a day, month, year, or more, so you'll need to research until you feel comfortable investing in this business or product. Your goals will determine the quality, time, and effort spent on research. If your goal is to start in the home, but grow into a larger company, then you'll want to spend considerable time researching and developing a business and marketing/sales plan.

Think of market research as a way to develop a profile or resume of your average customer, how many of them are in a given area, and if their numbers are growing or shrinking. You can find Demographic information on your prospects, such as age, income, sex, family, location, occupation, or Psychographic information such as life-style, hobbies, and buying motives. The more you know about your customers, the better you can develop marketing communication materials that meet their needs. Market research should also tell you what the "experts" predict for your type of product or service, and what the competition is offering and how they reach their customers (Yellow pages, flyers, ads, telemarketing).

There's a number of ways you can use a computer to get research information. One method for gathering industry information from magazines, newsletters, and newspapers is to access an on-line database. For example, Compuserve allows you to directly access several research databases, such as the *Business Dateline* for articles from local and regional newspapers and magazines. There's also a database of newsletters that you can tap for "insider" and specific information on particular industries and products. You access the information by subject word, author, company name, geographic location, or publication date.

For Demographic data, if your prospects are consumers (not businesses), Compuserve offers four different reports from CACI, a market research company. The Demographics Report, for example, offers general statistical information on an area, including age groups, household income, occupation, types of households, race, percentage of dwelling units that are owned and rented, the average home value, the average rent, and when the housing was built. (Based on the 1980 Census Report and 1988 updates for age, household income, and race.) The reports are based on averages, so the results are only an overview of the prospects in the area. Don't place too much emphasis on statistical-based research, especially if the number of prospects is small. (As Benjamin Disraeli once said, there are three kinds of lies—lies, damn lies, and statistics.)

You can also use on-line services like Compuserve to poll or survey prospects, consultants, and people already in the business in other parts of the country. Compuserve has many specialized forums where people with specific interests gather to exchange information, get help, and keep current in their specialty. For example, they have a special forum for people who work at home, one for people working in advertising and PR, an entrepreneur's forum, and many that specialize in computer hardware and software. To test your idea, you just have to leave some basic information about your product or service on the forum's "bulletin board." You often get excellent advice and comments that can help you refine and adjust your marketing and sales plan. There are many other electronic gateways to information as well. (For further information see Section 9, Reaching Out To Touch Someone, page 303)

Another way to conduct research using a computer is to survey or interview prospects and customers by phone. There are several software programs that help you conduct phone surveys, but most are too expensive or specialized for home businesses. Instead, use spreadsheet software to create survey forms for recording the results.

Once you identify the characteristics of your best prospects, you can find lists of them in books, magazines, or from list brokers. List brokers will sell you the list in computer readable format (usually expensive) or as labels. No matter how you get your list, it's best to develop your own database so you can keep the information current and confidential, and be able to use it anytime you like. (For further information see Section 8, Money in Your Mailbox, page 267)

CHAPTER 55

CREATING A ROAD MAP

Now that you know who your best prospects are, you need to find a way to communicate the benefits of your product and service to them. If you need financing to start your company or to expand your marketing efforts to other areas, you should not only write a sales and marketing plan, but a complete business plan. Fortunately, several good software programs can help you quickly and thoroughly develop a plan.

These programs come in two different "flavors," spreadsheet templates and standalone programs. Template software requires another program to function, usually a spreadsheet like Lotus 1-2-3 or Microsoft Excel, while standalone programs don't require any other software to operate.

Two good choices for business plan template software are Business Plan Toolkit and Biz-PlanBuilder. The Toolkit is composed of templates for Lotus 1-2-3 (MSDos) or Microsoft Excel (Macintosh) spreadsheets, a business plan workbook, sample business plan, and "starter" business plan outline. "The templates guide users through the planning process so that even if they don't know how to write spreadsheet formulas or forecasting models, they can get professional results—in formats that bankers, accountants, and investors will instantly recognize and understand," says Tim Berry, founder and President of Palo Alto Software. *BizPlanBuilder* has templates for either Lotus or Excel, as well as a business plan outline booklet (also on disk for your word processor) that helps you develop a complete business plan.

If you don't have a spreadsheet like Lotus or Excel, or if you don't feel comfortable using one, you can use a standalone software program. VenturPlan, for example, helps you develop a business plan by guiding you through a series of questions. It handles the formatting of text and computation of any data. There's several versions specifically designed for different types of businesses, like retail, service, consultants, and manufacturing organizations.

If you haven't bought any software to run your business, you might seriously consider Venture. It not only helps you create a thorough business plan, but also manages the day-to-day operations of your company. Venture includes a business-plan builder (including a thorough sales and marketing section), word processor, spreadsheet, file manager, and general ledger. It also has a feasibility plan which helps you determine whether or not your idea is strong enough to pursue.

If you don't need a complete business plan, but you still need to create a very detailed marketing plan, there's THE MARKETING MANAGER. It's a very thorough marketing plan, although you might be put off by the heavy use of marketing "jargon." THE MARKETING MANAGER *is* a standalone software program that asks a series of questions and uses your answers to create a marketing plan. It also includes a text editor and a glossary of marketing terms.

If you aren't going after financing, you can probably get by with a simple, one or two page marketing plan that you create and edit on your word processor. It should include your marketing goals (how many widgets you want to sell or the number of customers you want to gain), a summary of the main benefits you are offering (including any benefits that are unique or that you're going to emphasize), your best prospects and their profile, how you are going to communicate with them (ads, letters, phone calls, etc.), and your marketing budget. Since it costs more to get new customers than to sell to current ones, be sure you continue to market to them. For example, you can use customer marketing "tools" like calendars or mugs at Christmas time, free samples, and plenty of follow-up phone calls, letters, and visits.

No matter what your research shows, never underestimate the power of an hunch or intuition. If marketing and sales was really a science, then most successful "fad" products like the Pet Rock would never have been developed and sold. You just can't accurately predict the true reaction of people to every product and service with research. That's why it's still so exciting (and profitable) to create your own successful product and business. It's also why so many businesses fail within their first three years.

CHAPTER 56

SHARPENING
YOUR MESSAGE

Once you have your business and/or marketing
and sales plan, you're ready to develop your
communication tools that "carry" your benefits'
message to your prospects. Your communication
"toolkit" includes everything you use in your
business that a customer or prospect comes in
contact with—business cards and stationery, as
well as brochures, ads, and sales letters. However you market and sell your product or service—ads, brochures, coupons, phone calls, or
letters— remember that it takes repetition and
time to break through the noise.

Today, it's much easier to create your own professional-looking marketing materials thanks to desktop publishing systems, and presentation and word processing software. (For further information see Section 6, Working With Words, page 155)

Writer's aids like spelling and grammar checkers, thesaurus, and stylebooks are also available to help you improve your writing. However, for most people, the objective of a home business isn't to do everything yourself. Just like doing plumbing, electrical, and carpentry work around the home, if you have the skill and desire and time, you might "do-it-yourself." If not, you'll probably hire someone to do it for you. Creating marketing materials like ads, brochures, flyers, and direct mail is the same. Without the right skills, tools, and desire, you should consider hiring a freelancer to help you. Even with a desktop publishing system, you still must be able to write clear, persuasive copy, design and arrange the elements (type, photos, illustrations) on the page in an attractive, eye-catching way, and paste-up any photos, graphics or illustrations. So it's important to evaluate your skills to determine what you can do, and what you need to contract out. Anything that improves the effectiveness of your marketing materials can be the difference between success and failure.

CHAPTER 57

MAKING THE SALE

Once you know who your best prospects are, where they can be found, what sales message to communicate, and have your marketing materials in-hand, you'll want to start contacting them. Contacting, selling, and following up with prospects and customers are key components of the sales process, and often the most difficult for people without sales training. All your research, planning, and marketing communication efforts are worthless if you don't properly and methodically follow up. Keeping in touch isn't just a courtesy, it's crucial to the health of your business. Perhaps the biggest reason for losing a client is not dissatisfaction with the product or service, but because they don't hear from you enough and think you don't care about them.

Many people still use 3 X 5 card systems to track and record prospect contact information, including salesmen for large companies, but manual systems have some major failings. One problem with cards is that you can only sort them one way. Either they're in alphabetical order by the name of the prospect, or they're by follow-up date or telephone number. If someone calls you back it's hard to find their card. Computer tracking systems can sort records almost any way you like, and even find cards by any of several alternative ways at the same time. Since it can take up to five contacts to close a sale, it's also much harder to keep up with a manual system.

The good news is that the vast majority of sales and marketing software programs are designed for tracking and keeping information on prospects and customers. The bad news is that the number of programs and features makes it difficult to compare, evaluate, and select one for your business. Although many of them have the same core capabilities, they often have other features that make them slightly different. Also, to attract broader sales, the same program is often sold as account management, lead tracking, personal management, sales management, and telemarketing software. So take a close look at the features you'll need to manage your business, instead of the category the program is sold in.

The minimum features you'll need to track prospects and customers are name, company name, address, phone numbers (at least two, for business and personal), source (where the lead came from), type (customer, prospect, supplier), the ability to schedule follow-up phone calls or letters, and a notepad area for additional information. You should also be able to get a number of reports—at least by name, company, source, type, and zip code. Being able to define and rename "fields" (address, type, and source are examples of fields) where the information is stored is important if you need to track anything particular to your type of business.

(If you're planning on marketing primarily through the mail, see Section 8, Money in Your Mailbox, page 267 for software and marketing recommendations.)

If you're planning on using a combination of the phone and mail, or if you're planning on using a variety of methods, including phone calls and letters, as well as advertising and public relations, then two programs are good examples of what to look for in sales and marketing software. Although these are excellent programs, you should always evaluate YOUR needs before you purchase one for your business.

The first, MarketMaster R/A, for Macintosh only, is very well-suited for most home businesses. The most outstanding feature of MarketMaster is that it helps you develop and automate a marketing strategy. It's not just a database of customer and prospect information. The first thing you do is plan the flow of sales events and their possible outcomes. Most programs will let you schedule one follow-up activity, but not a whole sequence of events like MarketMaster. It tracks prospects and customers in the standard ways, by name, company, address and phone number, origin, type, interest, sex, but also by lead status, or where in the sales process they are, which is automatically filled in. You can also create a number of reports based on this information.

Another good overall program for marketing, especially by phone, is Telemagic.

CHAPTER 58

INTERMISSION
A WORD ON EASE OF USE

Software must be easy to learn. Even people with very little background in computers should be able to quickly become proficient. Another "ease of use" consideration is speed. Every program functions great working with a few sample records, but the real test comes when you have a few thousand full ones. If it is too slow, a phone marketing program isn't useful during the actual call.

CHAPTER 59

SELLING BY PHONE

Of course, an easy to use program would be worthless without a wealth of features that support your phone marketing efforts. You'll need many "call management" features that make it easy for you to actually use the program while talking on the phone, and for quick and efficient follow-up. You will want support for automatic dialing with a modem, and headsets, important for hands-free operation.

The prospect call screen should be well designed and have multiple fields you can define for tracking information specific to your business. One nice feature is automatic branching, the ability to move to sublevels of a script with a single keystroke, depending upon the user's response. You should also be able to record details of the conversation in a notepad area. Better yet, the notepad should have automatic date and time stamping, a helpful time saving step extremely useful for tracking conversations. The software should also allow you to schedule a follow-up call, important in building long-term relationships by just typing in a recall date, time and optional call type.

Good software will allow you to send a follow-up letter with just a few keystrokes (after you've set up and written the "template" for the letter). Or quickly follow-up the call with a FAX, voicemail or electronic mail. Alarms are an additional feature that alert you to tasks waiting for your attention. When an alarm goes off, a brief message is flashed on the lower part of the screen.

There are a number of ways to find a particular prospect or record. A "Go to" selection will search for records by predefined Primary and Secondary IDs (usually a last name and company name), recall date, first record to call or the last record added. A handy "bookmark" feature will save your place if you want to return to the same record.

Another important feature is reporting capability. To group records together for special reports or calling campaigns. A filter lets you select records based on any of the fields, such as city, state or customer type using rules of logic, such as AND, OR, EQuals and Not EQual. In addition to a number of standard reports, like telephone usage, phone listing and scheduled calls, a program also lets you create custom reports.

CHAPTER 60

INTERMISSION 2
A FEW POINTERS

Compatability

No software program is an island, no matter how "integrated" it may be, or how many modules like word processing it includes. It should let you use your other programs with it. It's very easy to switch between your favorite word processor or spreadsheet and a good marketing program.

If you're selling a product, you'll also be interested in the accounting interface. The program should either provide an order entry module for programs such as SBT, RealWorld, Open

Systems and Sourcemate, or include the link if you already own the package.

It's important to move data between your programs, such as importing a new call list, or exporting the prospect list to a spreadsheet.

There are three ways to import data: files with all fields of fixed length, comma delimited text files and specific database files.

A good program not only grows with you, but can also go with you. If you're constantly on the move, a compatible version should be available for laptop computers. If you need to automate several people, it should support both local area networks (LANs) and Unix. It is best if information can be moved between IBM compatible and Macintosh computers.

Security

In marketing, your prospect and customer list is your livelihood. If you plan on hiring others to market for you, or have children around who might "play" with your system, it's probably a good idea to protect the information and prevent unwanted use of a program. There are security programs available on the market, especially for networks. A potential problem with lists or databases is their quality. Often they have duplicate, incomplete, or out-of-date records which need to be culled. A good program will find and eliminate duplicates with the same Primary IDs. Direct mail or list management programs usually have excellent features in this area for comparison.

Customer support

Don't just shop on price. You're going to invest a lot of time with your marketing and sales program, which means that you'll need solid support sometime down the line. Telemagic, for example, includes unlimited telephone support for six months and a bulletin board system (BBS) for getting questions answered. You can also purchase additional support that includes phone calls, a newsletter, and one year's worth of free software updates.

If you're unfamiliar with computers or tele-marketing software, make sure your dealer or consultant is well-versed in the program. A reliable local source of support can be invaluable in those critical times when you need immediate help.

Training

If all this information still didn't make marketing and sales clear, or if your appetite is just wetted for more, the computer can assist you in your quest for knowledge. Although there's not many good, inexpensive training programs in marketing and sales, you're going to see many more within the next few years because of the number of people starting home and small businesses. The computer is perfect for training, it's patient—ok, it might beep at you, but no yelling—and teaches at your pace, not that of the instructors.

CHAPTER 61

GETTING STARTED

Where do you start? Since marketing and sales provide the lifeblood of your business—new customers—you need to make it a strength as soon as possible. However, if you're like me, or most people who start home businesses, you probably already have, or will quickly get, one or two loyal customers who provide the bulk of your income. For any business, customer referrals and references are one of the best ways to market and sell your product or service. Usually, your loyal customers are more than willing to provide you with letters of recommendation that you can use in your flyer, ads, or show to prospects. Remember, as you gain more customers, your main advantage is SERVICE and PERSONAL RELATIONSHIP. Use the computer to help you build better relationships by reminding you to get in touch with your customers to send them Thank You notes after every sale, or to send a quick note just to say "Hi."

A computer can't turn a bad marketing and sales person into a good one. Only you can do that. For example, if you use one of the "standard" letters that come with the sales software, be sure to rewrite it to fit your personality and style. If it sounds phoney to you, it'll surely sound phoney to them. Also, as you eagerly expand your business, be aware of the 80/20 rule in sales. It states that 80% of your sales comes from 20% of your customers. Yet in many large corporations, the 20% are ignored or taken for granted, or the other 80% are treated like second-class citizens. You can't afford to do either. One unhappy customer can quickly soil your reputation. Even a small customer can talk to your best customers. Let the computer help you take care of all 100%.

So how do you start? The main difference between success and failure in sales and marketing is that successful people aren't afraid to make the call, send the letter, knock on the door, or invest in an ad—to them it's an adventure, and it's fun. They also know that not every sales attempt will succeed. They expect refusals—but they also expect a lot of sales. So put on your Marketing and Sales Hat, turn on your computer, and start the hunt for your first customer. And smile, because it's fun when you're driving the business.

RESOURCES

Recommended Books

Guerrilla Marketing Attack, Jay Conrad Levinson, Houghton-Mifflin

The One Minute Sales Person, Spenser Johnson, M.D and Larry Wilson, Morrow

How to Master the Art of Selling, Tom Hopkins, Wamer Books

Growing a Business, Paul Hawkins, Fireside

Marketing on a Shoestring, Jeffrey P. Davidson

Phone Power, George R. Walther, Berkley Books

Do-It-Yourself Marketing Research, George Breen and A.B. Blankenship, Adweek Books, 1-800-3-ADWEEK

Business Plan Template Software

Business Plan Toolkit, Palo Alto Software (800-336-
5544)

BizPlanBuilder, Tools for Sales (800-442-7373).

VenturPlan, Venture Software (617-491-6156),

Marketing Plan Software

The Marketing Manager, MarketWorks, Inc (415-924-2117) .

Sales and Marketing Software

MarketMaster R/A, Breakthrough Productions (619-281-6174) (for Macintosh only)

Telemagic, Remote Control (800-992-9952)

Business Management Software

(includes business plan templates)

Venture, Star Software Systems (800-242-7827). It not only helps you create a thorough business plan, but also manages the day-to-day operations of your company

SECTION 9

MONEY IN YOUR MAILBOX

CHAPTER 62

YOUR INTRODUCTION
TO MAIL ORDER

Mail order tools used properly can enhance and expand a home-based business. While mail order is a business in itself, any home-based business operating on either a local or nationwide basis can make use of mail order tools to build and better service their customer base. The mail is the perfect tool to keep in touch with your customers through bulletins and newsletters, sales brochures on new products and other informational text.

To fully understand the impact of mail order in your business, consider the following: Con-

---

sumer mail order sales reached $73.6 billion in 1988. If you add business purchases to that, the figure soars to $126.6 billion. This is according to Marke/Sroge Communications, a catalog consulting firm in Chicago. Also, consider that more than 12 billion catalogs were mailed to consumers in 1989 and the number of people who shopped by phone or mail in the last year reached nearly 92 million, according to the Direct Marketing Association.

My company is presently involved in selling business opportunity materials through the mail and makes extensive use of mail order tools to expand and keep our existing customer base. This chapter makes liberal use of tips of the trade I utilize in my own company since my needs are similar to many other small and home-based businesses.

Since most of my business consists of communication through the mail, with only limited contact by phone, and absolutely no contact in person, it is imperative that I make the best use of mail order to continually expand and build my business.

CHAPTER 63

BUILDING YOUR LIST

Mailing lists or customer databases including mailing information are the basis of utilizing mail order tools in your small or home-based business. Any mailing lists you plan for your business will begin with your existing customers. After all, they are already familiar with the products and services you provide and are proven buyers.

Your customer lists are often referred to as in-house lists. These are often your company's most precious commodity. You should always mail your best offers to this list and mail frequently. Your customer lists can also be leased through a list broker at considerable profit to you.

Aside from existing customer lists, you will probably also want to maintain an inquiry or responder list. These are sometimes referred to as mail response lists. This is a mailing list of people who have inquired or responded to your advertising or offer and are interested in becoming a customer. This is developed through references from your valued customers, inquiries to classified or display advertising and other methods.

While names in the responder list might not purchase with the first mailing, you should strongly consider mailing them at least three more packages over the next six months to attract their interest and hopefully, their business.

Both existing customers and a responder list are developed and maintained yourself. You decide when to drop non- or poor names on your list. The list names can be maintained together with various fields used to differentiate between purchasers and just inquiries.

To keep these lists current, mail to these names at least three times per year. Purge any returned address names regularly and check for duplicates.

The third type of mailing list is a rented or purchased list of potential buyers with characteristics in some way similar to your existing customers. These are names who have responded to another company's offer. Let's say you sell a catalog of baby furniture. You might lease a list of expectant or new mothers. If you are a moving van company, you might want a list of homeowners with houses currently on the market in your area.

Rented lists are normally available on a one-time basis with an additional fee charged to reuse the list. To get around this, I often include in my promotional materials, a section for the reader to indicate their interest to remain on my mailing list. Otherwise, I will not be able to send this particular reader any additional materials.

These lists can be obtained directly from the company offering them or through a list broker. Standard Rate and Data Services, Inc.(3004 Glenview Road, Willmette, IL 60091), publishes the "bible" of mailing lists for both consumer and business use.

The problems with rental lists are as follows: incorrect addresses, often because of the age of the list; materials not sent when the buyer wants to buy, because the reader didn't specifically request materials, like they might if responding to an ad. There is a risk of sending them something when they are not ready to buy.

If I can catch their interest and retain them on my own responder mailing list, I stand a better chance of making a future sale.

A more important problem with rented lists is their applicability to your own business. Just because someone bought a product once, doesn't mean they'll buy it again. I have seen rental lists which are supposed to contain proven buyers, but in actuality, buyers of a $1 catalog, not the average $20 publication that I might sell.

CHAPTER 64

GOOD SOFTWARE
MAKES YOUR JOB EASIER

Software for mailing lists

Mailing lists are best maintained in a database-type software package. There are so many packages available that it would be foolish to recommend one over the other. Key concepts to consider in the selection of software include flexibility, with the accompanying ability to change the way information is organized; ease of use, if you are new to computers; interface with label and word processing programs, to allow you to generate labels and personalized letters based on your mailing list.

There are a number of software packages specifically designed to meet mail order processing needs. These have the advantage of eliminating the need to develop the database from scratch and the disadvantage of possibly being inflexible or not meeting exact needs.

Some software packages simply manage mailing lists while others offer complete turnkey systems to handle order entry, shipping, and accounting.

The first step in developing your mailing list is to establish what information you want to collect about your customer or potential buyer.

The following represents some of the types of information or fields which I use in my own databases.

The first group of fields contain the actual mailing information. They include:

Salutation-
(Ms, Mr, Mrs, etc. enabling me to personalize letters.)
First Name
Last Name
(NOTE: These are separated so I can personalize letters with Mr. Last Name and so on)
Business Name
Street Address and Apartment or Suite Number
City
State
Zip Code
UPS Mailing Zone
This is useful if you send UPS packages to your customer.

I will often run a report or specialized mailing list based on state or city considerations. To narrow down a geographic chunk of the country, I might run a list of all zip codes starting with 0 and 1 to reach many of the Northeast locations.

Phone Number
(Again, I may want to sort by area code.)
Lead
(This is the space where I can track how they heard about our company, what magazine issue and the like.)
Date of Inquiry
Date of First Purchase
Date of Last Mailing
Date of Last Purchase
Amount of Highest Purchase

These fields help me further select names for specialized mailing lists, offers or sale of lists to others. I may want to target recent inquirers, large purchasers or another feature.

By tracking the date of last mailing, I can periodically obtain the names of people due for another mailing. This eliminates the requirement to send a new promotional package to each and everyone on my mailing list, a daunting and expensive task.

Other fields are more specific to the service or product you sell. Examples include:

Special interests
(This can be developed through questionnaires, knowledge of the advertising they initially inquired from, products they have bought from you in the past, or special interests they note in their inquiry back to you. This is useful for sending specialized mailings based on only a section of your product line.)

Computer Operating System
(If you are selling computer software or computer related products, it would be helpful to know if they are using a MS-DOS, OS/2, or MAC computer system. Other pieces of information about their computer could be maintained such as size diskettes desired, laser or dot matrix printer, or whatever is relevant to your service.)

When deciding on mailing list software, first consider how the information will be used. Possibilities include generating personalized letters and correspondence, printing out various types of labesl, analyzing trensd and responses to advertising and inquiries or monitoring responses to specific ads and catalogs. You may also want the ability to purge duplicates or match entries based on similar address or phone number. This will help reduce your printing and postage costs by eliminating the problem of sending oodles of catalogs or brochures to the same home or business. It can also keep you from annoying a potential customer with overkill.

The ability to track purchase levels of a customer can also be important. This is helpful for tracking small or big spenders for select mailings. You will also want the ability to track special interests or buying habits of customers. These last two items are useful in the following application:

Let's say you want to mail a specialized brochure to customers spending at least $100 who are interested in purchasing real estate books, as opposed to the more generalized business opportunity books you sell. By utilizing these features, you could generate a specialized mailing list meeting your specific and select needs.

Many companies make more money leasing or selling their existing mailing list than they do selling their own products. Your mailing list management software should have the ability to export all records or select records to a disk, preferably in zip code order.

You should investigate the number of records the program can handle and decide if that will meet both your current needs and future growth.

Consider the capacity for number of items you carry. Can the system cope with your unique needs, such as size or color differences?

How does the system handle product numbering? Will it conform with your current product numbering scheme?

Are the reports which can be generated suitable to your needs and can you customize your own?

Label software

Many list management, database and word processing programs will meet your label generation needs. It is nice if the same software you use for your mailing lists and shipping will also print out labels. This eliminates the need to go to another piece of software to handle this.

Shipping software

Shipping software is discussed in detail in Chapter 66, Letting Your Computer Fill Your Orders, page 285.

CHAPTER 65

MAKING YOUR MAILING

Your mailing piece represents you and the image you are portraying for your company. Use the best printer you can. I strongly recommend a laser printer to create this image. Many word processing packages now support desk-top and graphics features and should be used liberally to create your promotional pieces.

If you do not have graphics software, you might work with your local printer or graphic artist. Both of these sources have volumes of clip-art, both computerized and on paper, which you can incorporate in your sales material.

Components of your promotional piece

The components of your mailing piece should include the following:

Sales letter

If the reader looks at nothing else, they will often at least scan the cover letter.

The sales message represents the most important part of your mailing piece. Your sales letter can be printed on your letterhead or you can start with a key sales phrase like, "Don't Miss this special offer"...and then jump right in with your sales message.

If a sales letter does nothing else, it should sell!, sell!, Sell!.

The four steps which should be addressed in your sales letter are: 1) Getting attention, 2) Getting the reader interested in what you can do for them, 3) Making the reader desire the benefits of your product, 4) Demanding action and asking for the order, TODAY!

A sales letter can be printed on one or both sides of a page but should rarely go beyond two pages. The exception is if the sales letter is taking the place of a brochure or informational piece and you need an adequate amount of space to describe your product or service.

Be sure to include a guarantee of some sort. This will tremendously increase your business and lend a degree of credibility to your mail order offer.

Sample guarantees might include a 15 or 30 day money back guarantee or an offer to pay later, say after a specified period.

Another option is use of a free offer or special item to be included if they spend a minimum purchase amount or respond in a specified amount of time. Novelty or throw away items are great for this as they increase the perceived value of your offer.

Brochure or information on your product

This can often incorporate an existing brochure or product description you have on-hand. If you sell an inexpensive or hard to describe product, this might be a spec sheet or color picture of your product.

The Coupon or Order Form

The order form can be incorporated directly with your sales literature or be maintained as a separate piece of paper or coupon. Place a label with the customer's name and address on the order form making it easier for the person to place their order. This increases your handling time of each mailing piece but will increase your orders.

Keep the order form as short as possible but in direct proportion to the common number of items typically ordered from your customers.

Return or reply envelope

You must make ordering as easy as possible. The return or reply envelope implies the credibility of your company. Your printer can prepare these inexpensively. The normal size is a

#6 1/4, which is a small envelope measuring 3 1/2" X 6".

You might also consider using a business reply envelope. This is the same size envelope but is pre-printed with the business reply information received by the United States Postal Service. A customer or responder using this envelope pays no postage and this will increase the number of orders you will receive.

You must obtain a business reply mail permit from USPS. You pay the first class postage plus an additional 5 cent handling charge per piece. Your printer can print up your business reply mail envelopes.

An effective direct mail piece should: 1) Present your information well, 2) Offer a free gift or novelty item, 3) Provide some guarantee making the offer risk-free.

Make sure your mailings always present your materials professionallyy. Have them designed if you don't have adequate equipment. Proofread everything and use a spell checker very liberally.

Going the postcard route

Sometimes you want to do a mass mailing to reach a large group of potential or current customers, but don't want to incur the heavy expense of postage and printing. Some companies have found the postcard method very effective. At today's postal rates, a postcard can be sent for 15 cents.

Instead of sending a complete package to everyone on your mailing list, you send out a preprinted postcard (or handwritten for the personal effect) advertising a new product or whatever it is you want to get across and then asking the reader to return the postcard or call to indicate interest or to receive complete information. This is also a great option for announcing sales or a new customer service number to your loyal customers.

CHAPTER 66

LETTING YOUR COMPUTER FILL YOUR ORDERS

Link your mailing list with a system to track incoming orders, inquiries and fulfillment of orders. Use the information to get repeat business, track back orders, review which items are most popular, and other useful tasks.

The software you select to handle order fulfillment and order tracking should work in conjunction with your mailing list program. This means the customer data you collect in the mailing list program or module should directly interface with the order fulfillment software.

This is possible in several ways:

1) Choose a software package that handles both mailing lists/list management and order fulfillment.

2) Choose a software package that is compatible with a popular format, such as Dbase or Fourth Dimension so that records can be directly imported and exported between the two programs.

Consider what you want your order fulfillment software to do for you. Here are some of the possibilities:

Handle orders as they come in by phone
Provide inventory control features
Create invoices and compute shipping charges
Track COD, credit cards and refunds
Print shipping labels and packing slips
Handle taxable and nontaxable items
Generate personalized letters and order forms

The complexity of the package you select depends on how you plan to use it. This is dependent on a number of factors involving the particular needs and size of your business. Don't forget that the software must not just meet today's needs but be flexible and expandable to meet your future needs.

How many orders do you want to handle with this software?

How do you number your products today and are you flexible about changing the numbering scheme to conform with the software's limitations?

How many different products do you offer now and plan to offer soon?

Do your orders primarily come in by phone, mail, walk-in or some other method?

What kind of printer will you be using—laser, dot matrix?

Do you need a multi-user system to handle multiple order takers?

Must orders be entered as you take them or entered later in a batch?

What is the maximum number of items a customer might order?

The software package you select to produce reports should note popular items, track repeat customers and track back orders.

CHAPTER 67

KEYING
YOUR ADVERTISING

It is important to know where responders to our advertising are coming from, where they saw us, and whether they actually purchase our product or service after they inquire about it.

If our responders will be responding by mail, we can code our return address with the magazine and issue they are responding to. For example, John Doe Company-AT88, 400 Main Street. The AT88 might refer to a particular issue of a specific magazine.

If our responders will be responding by phone, we must ask the caller where he saw our advertising or heard about us.

CHAPTER 68

DECIDING HOW TO MAIL

Most of your mailings will go out First Class. At the time of publication, First Class is .25 for the first ounce. Be sure to mark your envelopes First Class, if you use this method, since this adds a degree of credibility to the person deciding whether or not to open your envelope.

First Class mail is generally delivered overnight to locally designated cities, two days to locally designated states (distances of up to 600 miles), and three days or more for longer distances. First Class mail is forwarded when the addressee has moved.

Fourth Class mail (Parcel Post) is designed for packages weighing one pound and can be insured. This service may take up to eight days for coast-to-coast delivery. If time is critical, you can send your packages First Class Priority Mail.

Priority Mail is First-Class Mail weighing more than 12 ounces with a maximum weight of 70 pounds. This is useful for sending packages when time is of the essence.

Second Class Mail is used by publishers and registered news agents who have been approved for second-class mailing privileges. The general public uses the single piece third class rate for magazines and newspapers.

To reduce your postage costs, consider Third Class Mail. There are several types of Bulk Business Mail including single piece, bulk mail and presorted. There is usually no advantage for small mailings to send single piece since the price is the same. If you are enclosing more than five pages or more than one ounce in your mailing, Third Class single piece is often 10 to 30 cents cheaper.

Bulk business mail, which is pre-sorted and specially handled, can be confusing at first. It involves sorting in categories based on zip code, carrier route, state, and other factors for increasingly lower postal costs. An annual fee and permit is required for Bulk Business Mail. Each Third Class bulk mailing must consist of at least 200 pieces. All pieces must be similar, i.e. all letters, all flats, or all parcels. To give you an idea of the price difference, at postage rates in effect today, a basic pre-sort letter will cost 16.7 cents, while letters sorted to a five digit zip code can go out as cheaply as 13.2 cents...a considerable savings from a standard 25 cent letter, especially when the difference is multiplied by the number of pieces.

Bulk business mail is also a good option when sending many packages out, for example, to fill orders. The current basic bulk rate package is 48 + 6.6 cents per pound/per piece. So, a one pound package would be .55 whereas a package sent First Class Priority Mail weighing 1 lb would cost $2.40.

Other presorting options include Presorted First Class and Zip + 4 First Class which each save about four cents per envelope.

Postal meters can be rented from Pitney Bowes or other sources. Postal meters can not be owned by your company due to postal regulations. You pay for your postage in advance and bring your meter to the post office to add additional postage. Newer models allow you to maintain a credit account and obtain additional postage over the phone through radio contact with your meter. The cheapest meter from Pitney Bowes rents for about $16 per month.

You should also obtain a good scale, which measures by the ounce or less. You will be surprised how one sticker or a slightly heavier weight paper will bring your mailing to the next postage level. Experimenting as you plan your mailing will help you monitor postal costs.

Be sure to weigh the envelope you are including in the mailing. On average, you can mail five pieces of paper and an envelope for the lowest rate, .25 (at present).

The United States Postal Service offers a number of publications on business mail. Many are part of a series called Creative Solutions for your Business Needs. Write to them or stop in your local post office for a list of brochures and publications.

CHAPTER 69

PREPARING YOUR
MAIL ORDER CAMPAIGN

You are now ready to plan your first mail order campaign.

As a sample product for this discussion, let's imagine we have developed a specialized software package that provides a complete mail order processing turn-key system. It handles everything from list management and advertising tracking to order fulfillment, shipping and invoicing.

Our first consideration is to decide what the potential market for this software is. Hopefully, we began to look at this prior to beginning to develop the software, so we should have a good idea of its relevance to our potential customers.

We have made this software both easy to use and flexible with growth capabilities built in. Since some of our potential customers are more experienced computer users, we built in the flexibility for the user to design and generate more personalized reports, interface with a large number of software packages and make full use of the computer's memory.

Our potential customer has or is planning to market their product(s) through the mail and wants to keep better track of this process. Other characteristics can be learned about our potential customer.

We have decided to use three methods to alert potential customers of our product. The first is to use our established customer list of people who have bought our other software packages. Although not directly related to mail order, these packages were designed to assist small business owners, a likely market for us.

Our second method will be to place small display ads in magazines targeted to our potential customer. This might include computer software magazines, small business magazines, like *Entrepreneur*, and mail order magazines. Responders to this advertising will be entered into our mail list software and then sent appropriate materials.

Our third method will potentially be the most expensive. This will be leasing several mailing lists from a list broker. The expense will not come necessarily from purchasing the list, but from the postage and printing materials required to send out thousands of promotional packages. Let's say we decide to lease the following list types:

1) A list of subscribers to a magazine who have expressed interest in mail order. This will have the disadvantage of including names who are not actually using mail order, those who don't have computers, and don't plan to; and those who already have mail order software packages.

Since we know that a large volume of small businesses don't have specialized mail order software today, and we hope that these small businesses have capitalized on the decrease in cost this past decade for computers, we take the chance that many of these names have purchased computers or may consider it when they know they can buy specialized software like ours.

2) A list of small business owners who have ordered any computer software package originally advertised in an *Entrepreneur*-type magazine. Again, this targets the small business owner, a market we feel is most receptive to our product. Other characteristics of this list include the knowledge that these people are willing to order a software package through the mail and respond to magazine advertising. This

is important since many people go to a computer supply house or store to purchase their software and at least for now, we will only be marketing our product through the mail. In addition, since our small business owner originally responded to an *Entrepreneur* magazine type ad, we can feel fairly sure that this small business owner perceives himself as an entrepreneur and wants to grow.

Since our name has already purchased software, we know he has the magic item necessary to use our product—a computer.

3) A list of members of a direct mail organization with less than 40 employees. Again, this list is deficient in that we have no knowledge of their use or interest in computer programs. We know that these people are interested in direct mail since they have taken the time to join this organization and we know they are part of small companies because of the employee size limitation. Another deficiency is we have no way of knowing if we are reaching the decision maker for purchase of this type of software.

We use our own order software to maintain, track and ship to our customers.

Our next step is to create the promotional pieces. We create a sales letter which touches on our key selling points. We start by introducing our company, the length of time we've been in business, the other products we've developed in the past and why this product is different from other mail order software.

We tell the reader about the low introductory price available for a limited time. We back this up with a 30 day money back guarantee.

We sweeten the deal by offering them something extra, such as extra service support, the next update free, or maybe a selection of labels.

We include a four page color brochure we developed depicting software screens, sample reports and a breakdown of special features and specs for the software.

We include a coupon reinforcing our low price, our guarantees and our special free offer or gift. We also include a business reply envelope requiring no additional postage by our customer.

With our mail order package complete, we are now ready to send the materials to our mailing list(s), both our own and our rental lists, as well as to responders to our advertising.

All our advertising has been carefully coded so we can monitor where the potential customer saw our advertising. This will help us to narrow down which advertising vehicles are most appropriate to our needs.

CHAPTER 70

A FINAL WORD
ABOUT MAIL ORDER

Using mail order tools carefully—while keeping in mind the increasing costs of postage and setting up your mailing list and mail order software— will help your company expand and continue to grow and prosper.

The key to making the best use of the mail is to take full advantage of all discounts available from the post office. Contact them for ideas and information.

When purchasing or renting a mailing list, choose the best list you can afford and make sure it fits your target market. Often it costs more to pay less for less suitable names than to pay more for ones which more closely match your product. Remember the main costs lie in printing and mailing.

Keep a close idea on the contents of your promotional piece. A heavier envelope or sticker can bring you up over the next tier costing you 20 cents more per envelope...a $1000 budget item on a 5000 piece mailing.

Choose your mail order software carefully. Be sure to fully evaluate your needs before plunging in and buying software. There are many packages on the market so be sure to think long-term, not just immediate need.

Above all, remember, using the mail can make all the difference.

Keep mailing!

RESOURCES

List Management Software

A selection of companies offering list management software includes:

Data*Easy PC Mail Order Systems, Data Consulting Group (415) 883-2300

DDI*Mailbag, Data Directions Inc., (708) 647- 2222

Doctor Data, Doctor Data Software (602) 246- 8907

Arclist available, Group 1 Software (800) 368-5806

The Mail Order Wizard, Haven Corp. (312) 869-3434

Home Business (for the Mac), National Tele-Press (800) 448-0988

Label Software

Labelpro works directly with Avery labels and is available from Avery Products, 818-915-3851.

Mail Order Fulfillment Software

Software packages to handle mail order fulfillment include:

Data*Easy PC Mail Order Systems, Data Consulting Group (415) 883-2300

Mail Order Wizard, Haven Corp, (312) 869-3434

Pony Express, specifically shipping software, from Melisco Marketing, (913) 642-5005

Bulk Mailer+ for the Macintosh, Satori Software (206) 443-0765

Further information on postal rates and requirements

More information is available in the USPS publication, *Third Class Mail Preparation.*

SECTION 10

REACHING OUT
TO TOUCH SOMEONE

CHAPTER 71

LEARNING TO TELECOMMUNICATE

If one revolutionary trend is responsible for the explosion of home-based entrepreneurial enterprises, it is the breakthrough in telecommunications. New developments in modems, FAX devices, low-cost 800 (WATS) numbers, and voice-mail systems have made possible new businesses with all of the technological bells and whistles once reserved only for full-sized corporations with large staffs and giant facilities. Now small- and home-based businesses can effectively compete with larger companies.

CHAPTER 72

---

800 NUMBERS

A WORD FROM JULIE JOHNSON

An 800 service offers exciting opportunities to small and home-based businesses. Formerly available to only for the largest companies, 800 service can now come to the smallest company via your home phone or business line.

Many long distance carriers are even marketing this service to the parents of college students as an alternative to collect calls. Introduced in 1986, business line-type services offer your small or home-based business the op-

---

portunity to offer 800 services over your regular existing business line or group of lines. These lines can also be used for regular incoming and outgoing calls. In the past, the line where an 800 call came in had to be dedicated to 800 service only, severely hampering the small business.

Today, most every long distance carrier offers this type of service including AT&T through its Readyline product, MCI through its Businessline service, US Sprint with FONline, and many other smaller and regional carriers. Telecom USA is the least expensive, charging only $2 per month.

All three carriers offer service from the United States, Puerto Rico and the Virgin Islands. MCI and US Sprint now offer this service from Canada, England and other European and Far East Countries.

Most carriers will allow you to list your 800 number through AT&T 800 Directory Assistance (800-555-1212), permitting you a further advertising medium. Many 800 users choose not to list their number to save costs, and only give out the 800 number to select customers. These might be customers doing a substantial amount of business, customers paying a membership fee or customers in very distant geographical areas.

If a home-based business wanted to market herbal food products through national advertising and suffered a poor response rate using a local office number, advertising an 800 number could change that. Allowing existing and potential customers to call toll-free at no cost to place an order might bring more business. A recent AT&T survey showed that 75% of shoppers were more likely to do business with a company with an 800 number than one without.

After business hours, 800 calls could be routed to an answering machine or service. The local telephone company makes no distinction between these calls and other incoming calls.

800 service is extremely popular because of its low monthly cost. Major carriers charge between $10 and $15 per month for the service plus a per minute charge for each call. This per minute cost, also known as usage cost, is only a penny or two higher than what it costs a customer to call. The cost per minute depends on the time of day and day of week but is about 24 to 28 cents during regular business hours.

Access from specific states and area codes can even be blocked. This allows a home business to only pay for the calls it wants to receive. For example, an East Coast company only licensed to sell product east of the Mississippi can block all area codes west of the River.

The key disadvantage of business-line type services is that an incoming 800 call cannot be distinguished from a regular business call. This can be a problem if both local and 800 numbers are advertised for customers to call.

Because of the added cost of an 800 call, a business may want to handle the call differently. This might mean talking for a shorter period of time or only getting an address and mailing information.

A small company selling business opportunities advertised their 800 number in magazines aimed at entrepreneurs and found that many callers not particularly interested in the service called strictly because of the 800 number. They would often call, asking for referrals or educational information. They wouldn't have done so if they were paying for a long distance call.

Obviously this may give the small company the option of trying to sell the caller products and services. But this is of questionable value to a small business with a low budget for communications and advertising costs.

Some examples of useful applications for this type of service include:

1) A home-based business selling consumer products through the mail advertising an 800 number to place orders;

2) A consultant offering an 800 number to select customers to offer advice and support;

3) A business opportunity specialist providing his "secret" 800 number only after a customer actually signs up for service;

4) A local financial services consultant (with a customer base in one state) blocking all area codes except for area codes within the state he services, only paying for calls in that select geographical area;

5) A small business using an 800 number whenever advertising in an out of state newspaper since they get a better response than when advertising a local number. Also, by using an 800 number, they hide their actual location by not including their local area code;

6) A business selling financial services advertising an 800 number nationwide. Callers reach an answering machine and hear a three minute recorded message about the offer and are invited to leave their name, number and address for more information; and,

7) A small newsletter publisher advertising an 800 number to subscribers to report upcoming information applicable to the newsletter.

CHAPTER 73

A WORD ABOUT TELECOMMUNICATIONS HARDWARE

FAX

Facsimile machines are everywhere, in home businesses and large corporations alike. Also known as FAX, these nearly omnipresent devices transmit documents—including graphic images such as artwork, photos and signatures— around the block or around the world in less than a minute. And all with standard telephone lines.

Standalone vs. Computer cards

FAX devices fall into two categories, either cards installed in microcomputers or standalone devices. Each has advantages. Standalone FAX devices are the most popular. In fact, they are what most people picture when they hear the term FAX. Standalone FAX products contain a built-in scanner and, consequently, are useful for businesses that transmit documents already printed on paper.

Operation is simple. A user commands a standalone system to make contact with the FAX on the receiving end, then simply feeds in the document to be scanned, and transmits.

A FAX device housed on a card inside a microcomputer offers some useful advantages over the standalone unit. With a FAX card, the software first converts the text or graphics file into a format usable by the FAX software. Since documents already residing in the computer do not have to be scanned before transmission, their quality can be much higher on the receiving end. However, the need for a separate scanning device to handle documents not resident within the computer can limit some companies.

FAX cards offer another useful advantage over standalone systems. Since FAX transmissions received by a FAX card can be viewed on screen before printing, much greater security can be maintained over confidential documents.

A standalone FAX device automatically prints out a document for any or all to see. Users concerned with their natural environment can often read FAX transmissions without printing, saving paper.

Pricing

FAX prices have plummeted within the last couple of years. FAX cards have historically cost less then standalone units but the difference can shift the other way if a separate scanner must be bought.

Currently, standalone FAX devices can be purchased from $700 and up, while FAX cards cost from $499 up to $1,200, depending on the features and options. These devices can be purchased for significantly less through mail order dealers.

In combination with answering machines

An interesting trend in FAX today—both standalone and cards— is the mating with other technology. While many standalone FAX devices have always incorporated telephone handsets for use in initiating a call, some models now come with answering machines. FAX cards can even come equipped with data modems for telecommunicating with other microcomputer. In fact, one device called the Complete Communicator is— on one card that fits into a PC— a complete voice-mail system with mailboxes and call forwarding, a full-featured FAX card, and a standard data modem.

The drawback of having that much in one card or device comes when it needs servicing. For example, if a standalone FAX system containing an answering machine needs to be sent for repairs, the answering machine is gone as well. A small business should not gamble on one piece of equipment becoming such an important part of its day-to-day operation.

Options available

Another interesting trend in FAX technology is that as prices continue to drop, options become included in the basic cost. Today's FAX devices possess a stunning array of options from which to choose. Here's two examples:

Considered almost essential by frequent FAX users is a paper cutter. FAX paper comes in rolls and becomes unwieldy when a long message is received. A cutter automatically trims the roll of paper to page size for easy manipulation and filing.FAX paper, even properly trimmed, can be unwieldy, so many workers make a copy of the FAX on a plain paper copier before filing it away.

A "broadcast" option lets the user record multiple pages of a FAX, and then "broadcasts" it to many locations, even automatically redialing those lines that are busy. Coupled with delayed transmissions, "broadcast" FAX devices let users defer sending a FAX until a set time—usually when the phone rates go down.

CHAPTER 74

WHAT THE HECK
IS "E-MAIL"?

A growing method of keeping in touch with clients and customers is electronic mail. Also called "E-mail," electronic mail systems—both public and private—offer a cheap way to exchange information best served by written communication. Due to the nature of E-mail networks, users avoid the annoying game of telephone tag, responding only when it is convenient and after they have investigated an answer to the original query.

How E-mail works

Electronic mail systems "store and forward." This means each user receives an electronic "mailbox" on the E-mail vendor's mainframe computer. If a user wishes to leave a message for another user, he dials up the mainframe computer, composes the message and addresses it to the recipient. The computer then forwards the message to the recipient's mailbox where it sits until he is ready to retrieve his message.

Public E-mail systems

Electronic mail systems can be divided into public and private networks. Public systems are those you subscribe to. They differ from private systems only in geographic scope and pricing, not in features or functionality. All allow users to send messages to other individuals with mailboxes on the same system. Major vendors providing electronic mail include MCI Mail, Western Union, AT&T, CompuServe, Genie, and BIX.

These vendors have different ways of charging for services. For example, since CompuServe charges for on-line time it saves the user money to compose all messages off-line for uploading as quickly as possible. On the other hand, since MCI Mail charges only an annual fee for a mailbox and additional fees mail sent but not for on-line time, the user can take their time.

With so many systems , each has chosen to do things a little bit differently.

Gateways

Recently "gateways" for communications between systems have become popular so it doesn't matter which system the person you are sending to uses.

A gateway provides a link between different services so that users of one service can send messages to users on another. Gateways overcome the problem of different standards for different services. There are gateways, for example, between CompuServe and MCI Mail.

Although this makes sending messages to users of another system possible, it still requires using the naming and addressing conventions of the service you are sending to. Fortunately, new standards are emerging to alleviate the problem. The X.400 and X.500 addressing standards provide a consistent naming convention to allow users to send a message to anyone whose service uses them. Gradually this is becoming all services,

Until all systems utilize the same protocols, DASnet, based in Campbell, CA, lets users of disparate systems exchange mail (text) and binary (program and data). DASnet links internal corporate electronic mail systems with public wide area networks (WANs) and a wide array of electronic mail services. DASnet links ATT Mail, BIX, Connect, DASnet hosts, Dialcom hosts, EasyLink, EIES, GeoMail hosts, INET, Internet domains, MCI Mail, The Meta Network, NWI, On Tyme DASnet Accounts, PeaceNet/EcoNet hosts, Portal, The Source, Telemail hosts, Twics (Japan), Unison, UUCP, and The WELL.

Private E-mail systems

Private E-mail systems can be implemented in many different ways. Many network operating systems (Novell, 3Com, TOPS) include electronic mail systems. Third-party vendors sell programs designed to provide E-mail services across popular local area networks.

These E-mail implementations are often restricted to users connected to the LAN but most make provision for users who either work remotely or are calling to pick up E-mail from remote locations.

"Public" BBS systems

Users on a budget might consider the relatively new electronic mail networks based on bulletin board systems.

In the early days of the BBS, there was little compatibility among systems. Even those based on the same software did not share files or E-mail. In short, they weren't connected.

Within the last couple of years, several large networks of BBS systems have developed.

The largest, called FidoNet, is a collection of BBS systems across the United States and Europe. Currently about 6,000 users send messages from any one of these systems to any other within about two to three days depending on message traffic. Since there are so many systems, it's likely that there is one in any local community and it costs only a local phone call to be connected to FIDO.

Once the domain of hobbyists and hard-core hackers, FidoNet volunteers now routinely route hundreds of megabytes of message and E-mail traffic in the dead hours of the early morning when phone costs are lowest. In addition, most FidoNet nodes also carry several "echoes"—discussions—about almost any topic imaginable, from ecology to computers to cooking.

While FidoNet is the largest, it is not the only BBS network in the "network nation." Several others carry E-mail. These include RelayNet, Interlink, SmartNet, and Canada Remote Systems.

Private BBS systems

An interesting alternative to "public" BBS networks like FidoNet is your own private BBS system. For a small investment in time and money, business owners can set up a system that will allow both staffers and customers to leave messages, request service, or place orders. Several BBS systems are available. A useful point to consider with a private BBS is security.

The BBS for profit

Some business owners have begun to use their BBS as the basis for their business. Studies have shown that businesses that provide unique or difficult to obtain information will become increasingly important in the future as society moves further into an information economy.

Many BBS systems charge for access. These are very competently-run bulletin boards with multiple lines, real-time tele- conferencing, real-time multi-player games, and repositories of software running in the hundreds of megabytes. The systems employ a small minicomputer or several microcomputers linked together in a network. Connection to these monster systems is often at a fast, 9,600-baud.

CHAPTER 75

ELECTRONIC UNIVERSE

In addition to electronic mail services, several E-mail vendors also provide a wide variety of electronic data services. CompuServe, Genie, and BIX—to name a few—all offer far more than electronic mail. Known alternately as "discussions," "conferences," and "bulletin boards," these systems provide a forum in which users share information and viewpoints about an almost unlimited variety of topics.

News and professional information

Finally, besides electronic mail and bulletin boards, there is also a wide variety of news, weather, legal, scientific, corporate, and stock information available on-line. Indeed, these services can best be thought of as "information smorgasbords" with users able to pick and choose what they want.

CHAPTER 76

ANOTHER WORD ABOUT HARDWARE AND SOFTWARE

Most of the systems and services described in this section use techniques known as asynchronous communications which, for the most part, can work over ordinary phone lines.

Data is transmitted using a device called a modem. The modem converts the computer's digital information to a series of tones and clicks that the phone lines can handle. At the receiving end, a modem converts the information back so another computer can interpret it. Obviously, the modems must be able to talk to each other. Just like two people from different countries, modems must agree on a common language in which to communicate.

The modems must agree on the speed at which they will communicate. Speed is measured in either bits per second (bps) or baud. Bits per second is the number of bits transmitted through the phone line in one second. Although bps is often confused with baud by new users, the two are related but not synonymous. Baud is the number of "state changes"—from 0 to 1 or back—that occur in one second. Most modem devices are measured in baud. When modems first became cost-effective for small businesses, they ran at 300 baud. The standard modem speed today is 2400 baud, but 9600-baud modems are about to take over.

There are only a few languages which most modems use to talk to other modems. By the time this book is published, the rules are slated to change again. Users considering a modem purchase, especially a high speed device, should be careful when shopping to get the appropriate device for the job.

Asynch comm packages

The hardware that connects two computers—the modems and the phone line—is only one part of the equipment needed for two computers to communicate. Special software is required to tell the modem how to so its many tasks such as responding to incoming calls, dialing a phone number, and transferring files. Popular programs for asynchronous communications include Crosstalk XVI and Crosstalk Mk.4 from DCA/Crosstalk Communications and SmartCom III from Hayes Microcomputer Products.

When considering a communications program for your microcomputer, there are several things to look for. First, determine if the interface is comfortable to you. If not, you will spend many frustrating hours trying to figure out how to make it work, instead of spending your time communicating.

Next, does the software offer the features you need to do your work? Look for features such as a phonebook for numbers you call most often.

Does the program have a "script" or "macro" language to help you automate repetitive and boring tasks? Can you use the software to transfer files to and from the systems you will call the most? Many programs do not have a wide variety of file transfer protocols or terminal emulations.

Finally, are you buying too much or too little of a program, with too many or too few features? In other words, will you quickly outgrow your purchase or have you bought something you may never learn how to use. Take the time to understand the work you want to do with the software and you will be better equipped to make the right choice.

CHAPTER 77

VOICE MAIL
KEEPING IN TOUCH

One of the problems facing workers in a home-based environment is the difficulty in keeping track of phone callers. Home businesses usually do not employ receptionists to answer the phone. Every worker in a small business must juggle many responsibilities, and may not focus enough attention on answering the phone and taking messages.

Businesses can consider voice mail systems. Many systems serve as simple answering machines, but they can be far more. Usually a combination of a dedicated computer and a special card, VM systems offer the caller a selection of choices—a menu of options ranging from leaving a message to transferring the call to another extension to forwarding a call to another location entirely.

Benefits of voice mail

The benefits of voice mail to the home business are obvious. If it is impossible for home-based workers to be in their offices at all times, voice mail systems can facilitate communication between customers and the business.

Like other advances in technology, voice mail can be abused. Users prefer to speak to people. For one- person businesses, this may not always possible but should be the goal.

Equipment and costs

Inexpensive voice mail systems include Watson from Natual Microsystems, The Complete Communicator from The Complete PC, and Talking Technology's BigmOuth. These single-line systems sell for $199 to $350. Units that handle multiple-line systems start at about $1,100 and go up to $12,000 and higher, depending on the number of lines that must be supported and whether or not additional hardware is required.

CHAPTER 78

THINGS TO COME

Just as technology now allows the home business the freedom of advanced communication options in ways that were impossible just five to seven years ago, so will the products detailed here quickly be outdated. New breakthroughs appear at almost frightening speed. What new and exciting technologies will the future bring?

RESOURCES

Major public E-mail systems
MCI Mail
Western Union
AT&T
CompuServe
Genie
BIX.

Gateways between systems
DASnet, based in Campbell, CA (links ATT Mail, BIX, Connect, DASnet hosts, Dialcom hosts, EasyLink, EIES, GeoMail hosts, INET, Internet domains, MCI Mail, The Meta Network, NWI, On Tyme DASnet Accounts, PeaceNet/EcoNet hosts, Portal, The Source, Telemail hosts, Twics (Japan), Unison, UUCP, and The WELL)

"Public" BBS systems
FidoNet
RelayNet
Interlink
SmartNet
Canada Remote Systems.

Asynchronous communications Programs

Crosstalk XVI, DCA/Crosstalk Communications, Roswell, GA, (404)998-3998

SmartCom III (Hayes Microcomputer Products)

Inexpensive Voice Mail systems

Watson (Natual Microsystems), Natural Microsystems, (508)655-0700

The Complete Communicator, The Complete PC, (212)582-2635

BigmOuth. (Talking Technology)

SECTION 11

MAKING YOUR PRESENTATION

CHAPTER 79

PRESENTATIONS
WITH YOUR COMPUTER

The microcomputer provides a window into the world of data that can be shared with an audience in several ways. To the computer, text and images are just different forms of data, and, while it takes different processing techniques to handle each, once these techniques have been encapsulated into programs, the computer takes little notice of the differences. To the observer, however, the effects can be staggering.

In choosing what kind of presentation process you will use, you need to consider two main points: (1) your audience, and (2) your subject matter.

The subject matter will most likely determine whether or not you wish to do a dynamic or a static presentation. A static presentation would include presentation from slides or from overhead transparencies, while a dynamic presentation would depend upon animation or real-time viewing of the computer in operation.

If, for example, you were planning to teach people how to use one of the windowing interfaces for the computer, you would find it easier to explain some concepts, such as "point and shoot" ("clicking") or "dragging" by direct demonstration, rather than by static pictures. You would want to use dynamic techniques for such a presentation.

The dynamic techniques, which will be discussed in greater detail later, are real-time viewing of the computer screen during user interaction (either directly or using a projection method), and animated graphics displayed by the computer (again, either directly or using a projection method).

If you were planning to present data that did not require dynamic displays (where such techniques would only get in the way or might be disturbing to the audience), then you can use transparencies generated from either photographs of computer screens or printed by the computer. These materials could be composed by a paint package, by a desk-top publishing package, by a CAD (Computer Assisted Design), or by a graphics editing package.

As you can see, you have several options available to you, and you must first decide which application(s) are important to you before you can choose the proper hardware and software for your task.

CHAPTER 80

TYPES OF PRESENTATIONS

In static presentations the message is presented without the computer at the time of presentation. In a static presentation, the computer is used as a tool to prepare the presentation, but the media used (slides or overhead transparencies) are displayed using traditional means (slide projectors or overhead projectors).

Overhead transparencies

The most frequently used presentation materials in both business and education today are overhead projector transparencies. Desk

Top Publishing software, when used with laser printers and variable-sized (scalable) fonts, can produce high-quality overhead transparencies fit for use with audiences of any size.

Scalable font packages from companies like Bitstream and Soft-Logic provide fonts that can be scaled from 6 points to 120 points. For most 8 1/2" by 11" transparencies, 24 to 32 point fonts are quite satisfactory, creating both an image large enough to be presented to an audience of a hundred or more, while still leaving enough room in a single transparency for roughly 15 lines of 35 characters each. These scalable fonts can be incorporated into any word processing program, such as Wordperfect or Microsoft Word, and are readily available for any laser printer.

While these transparencies are usually only available in black on white, they can be dressed up by the inclusion of graphics images from drawing programs and/or CADD (**C**omputer **A**ided **D**esign and **D**rafting) programs, provided that the images are stored in a format accepted by your word processor. Formats such as TIF (**T**ag **I**mage **F**ile **F**ormat, or TIFF), PCX (PC Paintbrush screen picture), DXF (AutoCAD **D**ata e**X**change **F**ormat) and EPSF (**En**capsulated **P**ost **S**cript **F**ormat) are readily accepted by most word processors that handle inclusion of graphics produced externally.

While word processors offer better font handling and a wider range of font choices than most drawing programs, they cannot produce their own graphics. This makes you dependent upon a computer paint package or drafting package, if graphics will play an important role in your presentation.

Slides

When computers first became available, the early presentation packages were oriented to the production of 35 millimeter slides shot directly from the image on the screen. This technique is heavily used today, with improvements in the quality, colors, and resolution of displays. Graphic images produced on a VGA display are capable of considerable resolution and an incredible color palette consisting of 256,000 colors. You can create images of photographic quality on a VGA display.

The newest presentation packages expect the presentation to be made using the computer in real-time, letting the screens change at a predetermined interval of time. This means that your presentation will have to run like clockwork and will not allow questions until you have finished. If you want to maintain control over the time between slides (screens), you may still use an "old fashioned" slide show, with slides shot from your computer screen. If you choose this approach, you will be able to shoot pictures from any of the packages described in the section on Dynamic Presentations, but you will find this task requires a good close-up lens and high speed film (I recommend an ASA of 1000 or better).

As an alternative to shooting your own slides, you may be able to find a local service, such as Autographix, Inc. of Waltham, Mass., who will produce professional slides from your file. You might also check with a Walgreen Co. drug store if you have one near you. This Deerfield, Ill. based company's Media Center produces slides from files as well.

The cost ranges from $3 to $5 per slide. If you are inclined to do it yourself, you might consider obtaining a film recorder from Matrix Instruments, Inc. of Orangeburg, NY. With the multitude of computer displays currently available, the one size fits all display to camera adapter is no longer available. You may have some trouble finding one that fits both your display and camera, although with a good close up lens that can focus down to 1 1/2 feet or less, no adapter will be required. To avoid the problems associated with parallax (which makes a range finder camera shoot a picture slightly different from what you see in the range finder), use a single lens reflex (SLR) camera, which allows you to see the picture through the lens before you take it.

Dynamic presentations

You can create your own slide show on your computer's display screen. While this can make for some pretty impressive presentations, be aware of two major limitations of this approach: (1) audience size, and (2) timing the intervals between slides. If the audience is small (say five or less), you can use the computer screen for your projector, although for larger audiences, crowding around a computer screen is not the way to do a very impressive presentation. This problem can be solved with some expensive additional hardware.

CHAPTER 81

GRAPHICS EDITORS

There are different types of software that can be used to build the graphical content of your presentation. These are (1) graphics editors, (2) paint packages, and (3) Computer Aided Design (CAD) packages. The first are explicitly designed for presentations and may be limited somewhat in their ability to deal with sophisticated pictures. The second are built for drawing and may be limited somewhat in their abilities to automate a presentation. The third group, while actually designed for mechanical drawing on the computer, are capable of making some highly detailed line drawings which can be augmented with text, albeit with a limited number of fonts. It should be understood that most of these packages are geared more towards image processing and less towards word processing. If you want fancy visuals to punch up your presentation, these tools can create them for you, but if you want easy modification of the text portion of the presentation, these software packages are inferior to a good word processor.

Graphics editors

There are several graphics editors available today with differing degrees of power to create complex pictures. To use them effectively, some degree of drawing skill is required, unless you are content with pie charts, bar graphs, stacked bar charts, freeform charts, and whatever graphic images are included with the editor. Included graphics often consist of maps of the states, maps of some large cities, and miscellaneous stock images that the manufacturer thought to provide, such as borders, people, traffic signs, buildings, and monuments.

With any of the graphics editors, some proficiency must be attained before you will get really impressive graphic presentations. Even so, a graphics novice can put together a presentation made up of graphs, text and the "stock" images after a day or so of using the easier packages. With that in mind, let us look at some representative packages.

Boeing Graph

This editor is relatively easy to use and has much power but has significant limitations. It has several built-in formats for graphs, consisting of sixteen different two-dimensional graphs, thirty three forms of three-dimensional graphs, and twenty different three-dimensional stacked graphs. Putting together bar, line, and pie charts is a snap, especially if you just substitute your own data in the samples provided.

This editor will give trouble trying to turn your ideas into reality, due to the lack of available clip art and the lack of freehand graphics support. But if charts are your goal, Boeing Graph has some outstanding stock three-dimensional graphs.

Cricket Graph

This editor, which is for the Macintosh, has 21 fonts which come in multiple point sizes. It offers 16 built-in fill patterns that can be used in pie and bar charts, but it is limited to eight colors. While it offers ten different drawing tools, it is a tedious process to make a good graph. Once you have constructed a graph, it can be pulled, stretched, or rearranged (axis reversal). Since Cricket Graph has no three-dimensional graph capabilities, it is quite restrictive.

Graph-in-the-box

This editor is unusual in that it is a RAM resident program and therefore can be used with your spread sheet or word processor to capture screen images from these products for incorporation into a timed slide show. It offers some very effective canned graphs and allows the creation of good graphs, but it is confining in that it provides no icons and has no tools for creating your own drawings.

Harvard Graphics

This editor is probably the standard by which all other presentation packages are judged. It is consistently a best seller and is listed by *PC Week* as one of the top ten software packages in sales at present. If you are a complete novice, you can find several books on the use of Harvard Graphics. These guides are readily available in any bookstore or computer store and cover use for beginners, experienced users, and experts.

Harvard Graphics has lots of power for producing presentations. It has several standard graph templates on which you can change the background or foreground pattern, alter the colors, and add ready made drawings (called symbols), although you cannot recolor these symbols. For text handling, it offers several sizes of fonts which can be enhanced by drop shadows or included in shadowed boxes. The images you create can be incorporated into a timed slide show run automatically by Harvard Graphics.

GRAPHICS EDITORS OVERALL EVALUATION

(Editors costing $250 or more)

Using the results of the *PC Week* poll of October 30, 1989, the top of the line graphics editors for IBM compatibles ranked as follows:

1. Harvard Graphics 2.1 (Software Publishing Corp.)

2. Freelance Plus 3.0 (Lotus Development Corp.)

3. GEM Presentation Team 1.1 (Digital Research Inc.)

4. Graphics Gallery 3.0 (Hewlett-Packard Co.)

5. Diagraph 4.1 (Computer Support Corp.)

6. 35mm Express 4.1 (BPS Inc.)

7. Microsoft Chart 3.0 (Microsoft Corp.)

8. Draw Applause 1.1 (Ashton-Tate)

9. EnerGraphics 2.2 (Enertronics Research Inc.)

HP Graphics Gallery

This package actually consists of three tools: charting gallery, drawing gallery, and clip art. It can do all the standard graphs and simple chart creation that the other editors can.

In addition to the stock chart editing, it provides drawing features generally found only in painting packages. Using the drawing tools, you can create your own graphics or include graphics that are provided (called clip art). With the tools included in the drawing gallery you can modify the clip art graphics by pointing and surrounding them with a flexible cursor (like a hollow square). You can then redo the color or the fill pattern, or edit the graphic itself. Using similar tools, you can easily move or rearrange whole or partial clip art images, so that whole new images can be created from existing clip art. With the text creation tools, graphics based text can easily be overlaid on graphics images.

Naturally, complexity does not come cheaply, especially in terms of learning. Expect to spend more time learning to make use of these enhancements than you will spend learning the simple processes.

Lotus Freelance Plus

This editor is built to accept input from either a mouse or a keyboard. It has its own clip art and has some very powerful charting features. If you are planning to create your own customized templates, (templates are formats for displays or charts that can be saved and reused with new data at a later time), then this package might be for you. It has utilities (like many other editors) to import data from other software programs, such as Lotus 1-2-3 and Symphony.

In a recent *PC Week* user satisfaction poll, it outscored Harvard Graphics in this area and in its compatibility with more high- resolution graphics adapter boards. Freelance Plus has more drawing capabilities than Harvard Graphics, if you plan to create original graphical images, as opposed to relying on the exclusive use of clip art.

Microsoft Chart

This editor, from Microsoft Corp., was outscored by both Harvard Graphics and Lotus Freelance Plus in the *PC Week* poll. Although it contains all of the essential features of the other editors, it was regarded as harder to use than Harvard Graphics, Lotus Freelance Plus, HP Graphics Gallery and GEM Presentation Team (not covered here).

GRAPHICS EDITORS OVERALL EVALUATION

(Editors costing less than $250)

Using the results of the *PC Week* poll of November 6, 1989, the low-end graphics editors for IBM compatibles ranked as follow:

1. First Graphics 1.0 (Software Publishing Corp.)
2. Pixie 1.02 (Zenographics Inc.)
3. Graph-In-The-Box R. 2 V. 2.2 (New England Software Inc.)
4. VP-Graphics 1.1 (Paperback Software International)

Additional excellent Macintosh programs include Deltagraph from Deltapoint ($99) and Aldus Persuassion ($339).

General conclusions on presentation graphics editors

To put on a slide show, you can expect to spend anywhere from $150 to $750 for the editing software alone. When deciding on the package to buy, you need to seriously consider your needs. If you are going to have slides shot from the images you develop, then you will not require software that has slide show capabilities, so transitional effects between slides (such as fades, explodes, and the like) will not be of interest. Also, the ability to re-sequence the slide show will serve no useful purpose. This choice alone may allow you to get away from the high-priced products.

Further, if your presentations will consist of standard graphs and charts, along with text and a limited amount of art, you can also get along with the low-end packages. If you do not anticipate developing your own art, look for a package that can either grab screen images from other programs or can import clip art of some form and forget the fancier drawing tools. These two choices can save you the most money and reduce your learning curve most substantially.

CHAPTER 82

PAINTING AND DRAWING

If you expect to do presentations that contain more art work and charts than text, or if you want to embellish your slide presentation with some truly spectacular art work, then you should consider one of the painting programs. Paint programs, or drawing programs, are designed for this purpose.

On the IBM compatible side only HP's Graphics Gallery, which includes Drawing Gallery, provides true drawing facilities. Since the Macintosh was created for this purpose, more programs are available on the Macintosh side.

Paint, or drawing, programs are artist's tools and are geared for freehand drawing. They provide tools to draw straight lines, curved lined, squares, circles, rectangles and a variety of other shapes. To do this efficiently, you will need a mouse or a digitizing input device of some kind. While some paint programs accept input from the keyboard, trying to control the drawing of a curved line with the cursor movement keys is a true exercise in frustration. If you do not intend to purchase a mouse, I recommend you stay away from paint programs.

If, on the other hand, you are prepared to spring for the extra cost of a mouse (see the hardware section that follows), and you have a bit of an artistic bent, then a paint program may be just the thing to spice up your presentation.

Output from these programs differs depending on type. The crispest results can be expected from those that can output in Postscript, a language your printer and computer should share, or Postscript compatible, format.

You will find that most paint programs give you a number of drawing tools. Most packages represent these tools with icons (drawings of the tool, such as a paintbrush, spray can, eraser, and pencil). By placing the cursor over an icon with your mouse and "clicking" (pressing the appropriate mouse button), you can select the tool you wish to use.

To begin your drawing, you would want to draw an outline. By clicking on the pen (or pencil) icon, you select that tool. Moving the cursor to the drawing surface, you can move the pen and repeatedly click at points on the drawing surface. The paint program will connect these points with lines. You can select lines of different thicknesses, as though you were choosing pens with different sized nibs. Similarly, you can choose regular geometric shapes (circles, squares, rectangles, ellipses) by clicking on the appropriate icon. Clicking on two points in the drawing surface will place the correctly sized shape in the drawing.

Once you have an outline drawn, you may wish to fill part of the drawing in with a color. Selecting a color by clicking on the palette, you can choose a paintbrush, fill, or air brush (spray) by clicking on the appropriate icon. If you chose the fill, you only need place the cursor inside a closed area and click. All the area inside the lines will be evenly filled with the selected color. To exercise more control over the placement of color, you can paint with the brush just by moving the cursor from point to point. The selected color will be left behind, just as though you had passed a real paint brush over the area. Use of the air brush is identical, but a mottled pattern is left, much like a spray paint can or an air brush would produce.

Use of the eraser icon lets you erase lines and colors from the drawing area. Also, some packages have an "undo" feature, which allows you to undo your last action. Changing the placement of an image (or portion of an image) is done with cut and paste tools (usually scissors and a paste pot brush for icons). By surrounding the part of the image you want to place elsewhere and then cutting it, you can paste it elsewhere in the drawing surface. Some programs provide a relocate function (a hand for an icon) which lets you shift the surrounded area anywhere in the drawing area.

Copying a portion of the image is usually accomplished with the cut and paste feature. Some programs also let you turn the drawing or a surrounded section on its axis, while some may allow you to mirror an image around an axis, thereby producing a complete shape from a previously drawn half-model.

Most paint packages produce images which may be reused or included in future drawings. Several also come with clip art that can be brought into your own drawing (in whole or in part). These clip art images may be colored or filled from the palette of colors and fill patterns. When choosing a paint package, look for one that produces images in one of the widely accepted forms or has conversion utilities to create widely accepted forms from its own format. Also look for conversion utilities which allow inclusion of other graphics formats, so that you are not limited to the graphics and clip art produced by a single manufacturer. The most common file types are GIF (**Graphics Interchange Format**, basic format of the Compuserve graphics forums), PCX PC (**Paintbrush** screen picture format), TIF (**Tag Image File**

Format, or TIFF), frequently produced by scanners and desk-top publishing programs, LBM (DeluxePaint picture, also called Amiga IFF), SS Splash picture, MAC MacPaint picture, not available in color, PCC (PC Paintbrush brush), RIX EGA Paint 2005 oversized picture, SCx EGA Paint 2005 picture (x is a code indicating the resolution of the image).

Essential features of paint programs will be found in almost all of the current group of packages available. Those packages that have additional useful features will be highlighted.

DeluxePaint II Enhanced

This program, from Electronic Arts, has all the fundamental features and supports all video resolutions. It has conversion capabilities to import and export images in MAC and PCX formats. It produces files in its own format (LBM). It has sixteen fonts available in multiple sizes, so that you can add text to your drawings. With its "Gallery" function, you can produce your own automated slide show.

DeluxePaint has one very unique feature which permits you to create your own brushes. With this feature, you can select a portion of the display that contains a pattern you want to use to fill in a portion of your drawing. For example, if you were to clip a brush from a section of the display and then draw a straight line, the line would contain the pattern and colors from the clipped section you used as your brush. The clipped brush can also be rotated in three dimensions, making perspective drawing much easier.

PaintShow Plus

This program, from Logitech, comes bundled with Logitech's three-button mouse for an extra $20. It can import and export TIF, MAC and PCX formats. It produces files in TIF format. It only provides 6 fonts, but it does have slide show capabilities. It is quite similar to Mac-Paint, being completely icon driven. It provides all necessary functions and is easy to use. It also supports the Logitech Scanman Hand Scanner. It supports all video formats, including black and white on a VGA.

PC Paintbrush +

This program, from Z-Soft, comes bundled under the name Microsoft Paintbrush (in a stripped-down form) with Microsoft mice. It can produce PCX and PCC format images, but it cannot import any other formats. It provides 21 fonts in many different sizes and additional fonts and clip art disks are available from Z-Soft. PC Paintbrush + has two font types, bit-map and stroke. Stroke fonts, which are drawn with line segments look good in any size, while bitmap fonts begin to look a bit grainy as their size increases, due to their being mapped from individual pixels (picture elements).

A major weakness of PC Paintbrush + is its undo function. Most undo functions remove just the last image added. PC Paintbrush's undo removes everything done since you started using the current tool. This can be overcome by periodically clicking on the tool icon, but this is awkward and should not be required. On the plus side, a conversion program is available to convert color images to grey scale, for use with your word processor, and a variety of input devices is supported, including digitizing tablets, many scanners and the keyboard.

Splash

This program, from Spinnaker Software, supports only VGA boards and requires an analog RGB monitor. Because it is designed only for high resolution graphics, it is geared to producing images of photographic quality. It has the ability to blend colors or to change colors to shades of grey. It will produce images in SS (its own format) and TIF formats, but offers no conversion programs for other formats. It does provide a slide show capability. Splash can accept input from a scanner or from a video digitizer. Clip art disks are available, and Splash provides 13 fonts.

Splash offers on-line help (by clicking on the "?" icon), giving text information on screen to guide you through the use of any tool. Quitting the help function returns you to your drawing. A unique mixture of tool icons and pull down menus exists to draw your picture. If a tool can be used in a variety of ways, clicking on its icon will cause the pull-down menu to appear.

For the Macintosh

Although IBM compatible computers have made significant headway over the past few years, many still consider the Macintosh *the* computer for graphics applications. Excellent painting and drawing programs for the Macintosh include Canvas from Deneba ($189), Pixelpaint Professional from SuperMac ($389), Freehand from Aldus ($339), and Adobe Illustrator ($279).

Paint program considerations

When choosing your paint program, you should ask yourself the following questions:

* Is there a complete enough set of drawing tools to do the kind of drawing you plan?

* Does the program support the kind of video graphics adapter and display you have?

* Does it have an adequate selection of fonts and sizes for the text you will need?

* Does it support a sufficient variety of input and output file formats?

* Does it have a method for incorporating other images (screen capture, clip art)?

The package that has the most satisfactory set of answers will be the drawing package for you.

CHAPTER 83

COMPUTER
ASSISTED DESIGN

While the software packages previously described are adequate for the majority of graphics presentations, true draftsmanship can be achieved only with a CAD package. These software packages, which are superb drafting and mechanical design tools, create files in Auto-CAD file format or IBM IGES format. Because of the rigorous detail required for mechanical design, the drafting tools in a CAD package offer more specialized functions like spline and Bezier curves. Features like chamfering, filleting and tangents are commonly used. Draw-

---

HOW TO USE A COMPUTER

ing perpendiculars and parallel lines, along with finding midpoints and nearest points of an existing line are also available. Drawing a circle or an arc from two, three or four points is easily done with a CAD package, while the majority of paint programs would balk at this and most of the tasks just mentioned.

Although CAD programs can handle colors and three dimensional drawings, they are not truly designed for presentation graphics. But, if high quality mechanical drawings are needed in your presentation, no other tool will suffice. CAD programs offer greater precision than paint programs, plus more sophisticated zoom and refinement capabilities. This precision requires more computational power and better quality displays than paint programs, due to the heavy computational requirements and the fineness of lines drawn. You will require a specialized monitor.

Mechanical drawing is outside the scope of this discussion. Since sophisticated programs cost more than $1500 even from the discounters, it is too expensive a method to use just for presentation graphics (serious design use is required). On the less expensive side, consider Generic CADD from Generic Software ($125 - $350), EasyCAD2 by Evolution Computing ($170), or TurboCAD, by IMSI ($99). On the Macintosh side, *MacUser*, in their Fifth Annual Eddy Awards (March, 1990) selected Vellum, with its intelligent drawing assistant interface, MicroStation Mac by Intergraph, and

In-Cad by Infinite Graphics, the first package to bring true 3-D solids modeling and stereo lithography to the Mac.

CHAPTER 84

ANIMATING YOUR PRESENTATION

Until recently, the idea of animating a presentation with a microcomputer would have been considered pretty far-fetched. Today, however, there are software packages that promise to make full-screen animation possible and simple. One of these programs, Autodesk Animator (from Autodesk), sells for $299 and was awarded *PC Magazine*'s Technical Excellence award for graphics for 1989. In addition to animation techniques, it offers "tweening" functions, which permit the development of transitional frames to change one figure into another.

Another animation program, Show Partner F/X, from Brightbill- Roberts, sells for $229. Show Partner lets you incorporate images from other graphics software, such as Harvard Graphics, Freelance Plus or any Windows program. These images can then be edited and animated.

MacUser dubbed MacroMind's MacroMind Director at $445 "the key software for multimedia presentations on the Mac." Studio/I from Electronic Arts ($96) is another excellent program which "combines an excellent black-and-white painting program with frame-by-frame animation, sound, and sophisticated motion effects, even into the third dimension." Studio/8, a more recent release at $296, allows for eight bit, far more sophisticated, graphics.

While such methods are better suited to point of sale demonstrations than business presentations, the programs may become of interest if your home business develops advertising demonstrations.

CHAPTER 85

SOMETHING TO RUN
YOUR SOFTWARE ON

No software would be able to perform its designed functions if it weren't for hardware on
which to run it. In addition to a computer itself,
a video adapter card and display monitor are
essential, either to see what you have designed
before printing it on a laser printer, or to provide a photographable or otherwise viewable
image.

In the IBM compatible world, video adapters
and displays come in five modes: Hercules
(monochrome), Color Graphics Adapter (CGA),
Enhanced Graphics Adapter (EGA), Video

Graphics Array (VGA), and VGA black and white. The total number of colors available and the resolution (number of addressable points on the screen) increase as you go from Hercules to VGA.

In the Macintosh world you purchase a card and monitor based on the number of bits of video reference and whether you want black-and-white, grey-scale or halftone, or color display.

If you want to produce images for a laser printer, then any adapter can be used, but you can see what you are going to get better at the high end of the resolution scale. If you are going to produce images for slides shot from or viewed directly from the computer, then only high end displays are worthy of consideration, since the palette of colors is too small to prove interesting. In short, only EGA and VGA adapters on the IBM side, or 8 or 24 bit color displays are worthy of consideration for serious presentation graphics. If you can afford the difference in cost, go with the best, you won't regret it. Make sure that your paint program or graphics editor supports your monitor and card, however.

Scanners don't live in vain

If you are not artistically inclined and you want art in your presentation, you should either buy one of the paint or graphics programs that has clip art available for it. An alternative is to purchase one of many scanners. These devices, which range in price from $150 to $2500, can digitize an image (black and white or color) and put it in a file for your computer, usually in TIF format.

The least expensive scanners are hand-held and can scan an image up to 4" wide by 14" long. Side-by-side scanning passes produce images which you can piece together to get wider images, but you may want to go with a full-page scanner if you expect to process a lot of 8 1/2" by 14" images. Most hand scanners also come bundled with a paint program, usually Dr. Halo or PC PaintBrush for IBM compatibles, or Superpaint for the Macintosh.

A scanner provides an unlimited source of art for use in your presentations. Remember you may still need to edit the scanned image with a paint program.

Getting it digital

Another way of getting image input is the video digitizer board. You have probably seen these at county fairs, where you can have your face printed on a sweatshirt or some other surface. Such boards require a TV camera and a computer. Like the scanner, they convert image data into digitized information that can be stored on a diskette. Once digitized, you can edit and color it with a paint program. A good indication of the popularity of this board is the fact that a close-out mail order company recently bundled one with PC Paintbrush, the video software, and a slide show software package for $170, plus $6 postage and handling.

Still another method of obtaining graphics for your presentation is the frame grabber card. This device will be cost prohibitive for many but, for those who need it, the card allows the selection of a single frame or cell from a videotape to be converted into a graphics format usable in your presentation. Of course, you will also need a videotape machine.

Mice and other alternatives

As mentioned earlier, if you are going to use a paint program, you must have a mouse (or a digitizing tablet). A mouse, which moves your on-screen cursor in any of four directions, is a small object that you roll across your desk top. As it moves, the cursor moves in concert. If you don't have one for your paint program, freehand drawing is nearly out of the question (try writing your name across your screen in script with your cursor using only the arrow keys on your keyboard if you remain unconvinced).

Mice attach either through a serial port (also used for modem attachment) or have their own adaptor (a "bus" mouse). Which one you will want depends upon the number of available slots or number of serial ports you have and currently don't use. Prices range from around $70 to about $175. Many come bundled with a paint program, so check this option before investing in a separate paint program. Logitech and Microsoft make two of the most popular mice. Mice come with one, two, or three buttons (for "clicking").

An alternative to a mouse is a digitizing tablet, which looks like a slate and a pointer that looks like a mouse with cross-hairs. The pointer serves the same purpose as the mouse. The cross-hairs give you greater accuracy placing the cursor. With a digitizing tablet, you can electronically trace a picture laid over the tablet into your computer by running the cross-hairs over the outline, clicking as you go. There are also digitizing pens, where the mouse is replaced by an object roughly the size and feel of a pen. These devices are more expensive than a mouse, but offer more precision, if you think you might need it.

Getting it out of your system

Up until now, all hardware and software described has dealt with producing graphic presentation materials. Actual delivery of the presentation has addressed only transparencies and direct viewing of the computer screen. Since the computer screen is small, only a small audience can be served by direct viewing. If you have need to present to a larger audience but want to view the slide show under computer control, you have two options.

The first device displays the computer screen image in a transparent frame which is an LCD display. When used with an overhead projector, the frame becomes a dynamic transparency. LCD technology has only recently demonstrated effective color. Toshiba, the first to produce a color LCD display for a computer won't have them in production until late 1990. Even then, they will be expensive. So don't be fooled by claims for color from an LCD overhead projection device. Macintosh users may need a special device or hook-up to use these projectors.

Another shortcoming of these devices is their need for relative darkness to project a sharp image, especially if your slides have much detail. If your presentation is intended to train, you may have to keep the room dark enough that no one can take notes while your presentation is in progress. You should try these devices out under conditions similar to your intended use before committing the $1200 to $2100 they presently sell for.

The second device is much cheaper (usually around $200), but requires a TV monitor or TV projection screen. It is a board for the computer that produces RGB analog output and has an appropriate RCA jack. (Some VGA boards have the jack installed, since VGA produces a composite color signal.) This board lets you project your computer's output on one or more TV monitors, serving a very large audience. Of course, you depend on having TV color monitors on site for your presentation or you must have your own and carry them with you (a big expense). Note that some hotels have arrangements with local audio-visual companies to allow you to rent TV monitors. This can be helpful to know in advance if you do your presentations on the road.

CHAPTER 86

LOOKING FOR ARTWORK

Compuserve Information Service is a commercial bulletin board service, available almost world-wide. It contains several forums where people of like interest gather for the exchange of ideas. Among the forums, there are three that deal with graphics. These make excellent sources of graphic images and more extensive information on the subject of computer graphics. The three picture forums are PICS, ART GALLERY, and GRAPHSUPPORT for IBM compatibles. There is also a MacDesign forum. They form the largest computer art collection in

---

the world, consisting of more than 10,000 images. Other information networks such as GENIE have similar features, as do a number of free electronic public bulletin boards. (See the TELECOMMUNICATIONS chapter for further information.)

CHAPTER 87

BRINGING YOUR PRESENTATION TO LIFE

When designing your presentation, you should first build a "story board," deciding in what order the material will be presented and where graphics can be used to enhance comprehension. It is at this point that I usually remember the old adage "a picture is worth a thousand words" and recall that no one ever said "a thousand pictures are worth a million words". This reminds me that pictures can be very abstract and are often ambiguously interpreted. While a few well-placed pictures will dress up the presentation, they should be used only where they

---

enhance and never to the point of distraction. The subject matter will help determine what mix of words and pictures best help you explain it.

Having determined what words, pictures, and charts are required, decide how best to construct each frame of your "story." I use several tools: a graphics editor, a paint program, a CAD program, and a word processor. Each is better suited for one type of image than any other. The graphics editor is great for graphs and charts. The paint program provides all the pretty pictures. The CAD program is essential for mechanical drawings, electrical schematics, and architectural blueprints. Of course, nothing processes text like a word processor. Each frame is created with the appropriate program.

Since my word processor can include graphics from other sources, though I can only print in black and white, I often insert externally created graphics directly in with my text. This enters the realm of desktop publishing, but I often provide manuals, fliers, and handouts with my presentations.

Since I can shoot my own slides, integrating the several different formats is not a problem. If it were necessary to collect them so that Walgreens could run the slides, I could use the capture feature of my graphics editor to convert everything to one homogeneous format. This would also work if I wanted to have an automated slide show delivered by the computer, since the graphics editor has a slide show feature.

So, subject matter really does determine the optimal method. Once the method is chosen, the best tool for the job is selected and the graphic is created.

Delivery

Your audience helps determine how to deliver the presentation. If you expect to have dynamics in the presentation, such as questions during the presentation or changing the order in response to your audience, then transparencies are the only way to go. Slides are also flexible, but more difficult to alter in order on the fly.

If you can hold all questions until you finish, then you could run a computer-delivered slide show, provided that you don't have to speak or you have a precisely synchronized graphics and verbal presentation. While it is possible to actually control the transition from slide to slide from the computer keyboard, this can get in the way of your presentation. It also means that the keyboard will have to be well within your reach. For a small audience viewing the screen directly, you may get in their way. For a large audience viewing TV monitors, this works better.

Of course, if you are showing how to use the computer, then the best way is a live demonstration, especially when teaching use of a graphic interface. Here, slides just don't do the job.

Audience size and your presentation approach will determine whether you or your computer will run the show. If it is the computer, then audience size dictates the kind and size of the display(s) needed.

CHAPTER 88

FINAL WORDS
ABOUT PRESENTATIONS

The computer tools available for creating presentations are many and varied. They provide functions unheard of only a few years ago. Today, a home business can use computing and image processing power as powerful as many movie and TV studios had in the decade just passed. But before you go off developing the "Star Wars" of home produced presentations, consider that business presentations, even with these tools, depend on overhead transparencies first, slides second, and electronic frames third.

While it is projected that electronic frame generation will grow fastest of the three in the next few years, it is also expected that the order of priority will remain the same for several years to come. As a word of caution, before going too far afield, closely examine your business budget and then decide whether your presentations are going to sell the sizzle or the steak

RESOURCES

Graphics programs
  (Editors costing $250 or more)
  CorelDraw, Ottawa, Ont, (613)728-8200
  Harvard Graphics 2.1, Software Publishing, Mountain View, CA, (415)335-2000
  Freelance Plus 3.0, Development, Cambridge, MA, (617)577-8500
  GEM Presentation Team 1.1, Digital Research, (408)649-3896
  Graphics Gallery 3.0, Hewlett-Packard, Cupertino, CA, (800)752-0900
  Diagraph 4.1, Computer Support, (214)661-8960
  Draw Applause 1.1, Ashton-Tate, Torrance, CA, (800)437-4329
  EnerGraphics 2.2, Enertronics Research, (314)421-2771

  (Editors costing less than $250)
  First Graphics 1.0, Software Publishing, Mountain View, CA, (415)335-2000
  Graph-In-The-Box R. 2 V. 2.2, New England Software, Greenwich, CT, (203)625-0714

  For the Macintosh
  Aldus Persuassion, Aldus, (800)333-2538

Paint programs

DeluxePaint II Enhanced, Electronic Arts, (415)571-7171

PaintShow Plus, Logitech, (800)231-7717

PC Paintbrush +, Z-Soft, Marietta, GA, (404)428-0008

Splash, Spinnaker Software, Cambridge, MA

For the Macintosh

Canvas, Deneba, Miami, FL, (800)622-6827

Freehand, Aldus, (800)332-2538

Adobe Illustrator, Adobe, (800)344-8335

CAD programs

PCCADD, Generic Software, Bothell, WA, (800)228-3601

For the Macintosh

MicroStation Mac, Intergraph, (800)345-4856

MiniCAD+, Graphsoft, Ellicott City, MD, (301)461-9488

Animation programs

Animator, Autodesk, Sausalito, CA, (800)445-5415

Show Partner F/X, Brightbill-Roberts, (315)474-3400

For the Macintosh

MacroMind Director (MacroMind)

Studio/I (Electronic Arts)

Studio/8 (Electronic Arts)

FINALE

WHAT THE
FUTURE WILL BRING

CHAPTER 89

FUTURE TRENDS

Having completed our tour of the new wonderland computer technology offers to home offices, it is time to speculate on what the future will bring. Prognosticating is always a dangerous profession. A quick look at how far computers have come in a brief period of time illustrates the difficulty in predicting where they can go. There are a few highlights worth observing though.

ISDN will link home offices with each other and with special services

ISDN provides a high level of information transfer between a home office and a myriad of services as well as to other offices. The number of information services will grow with the spread of ISDN.

Imagine several offices connected with high speed information transfer. Even though these offices are geographically dispersed, they function as if they are in the next room from each other. Today, that ability would be too expensive, yet with ISDN it will become reality.

Many information vendors and services are waiting for the opportunity to establish effective telecommunications links with home offices. Today systems such as Compuserve and Genie cannot serve their needs, but tomorrow, with ISDN, this will change.

Several vendors already sell PC cards that are essentially "ISDN Modems"—cards that interface with an ISDN connection in the home or office.

MAC and PC computers will converge for all practical purposes

The variety of communications systems causes problems between users. In the future these problems will become a thing of the past.

New operating systems on the IBM such as OS/2 and Windows give the PC an interface more similar to that of a Mac. These interfaces make the IBM computer considerably easier to operate and shorten learning curves. Further, IBM has just entered an arrangement with Steve Jobs', the creator of the Macintosh, NEXT to adopt that interface to the IBM.

Several hardware and software utilities now make it possible to run IBM programs on the Mac.

Furthermore, new strategic announcements such as those between Microsoft and Apple to support the so-called "Royal" font format mean that users will have an even easier time exchanging documents from one environment to the other. The document created on a MAC will look exactly the same when displayed or printed out on a PC, and, of course, the reverse is also true.

A convergence of modem and signalling technology will allow all modems to talk to each other

Advanced techniques in "auto-bauding" or "feature negotiation" let modems figure out the best way to talk to each other without requiring the intervention of a human.

At the moment, 2400 baud is the acknowledged standard for asynchronous communications, but the emergence and acceptance of high speed standards by vendors of higher-speed devices will quickly up the ante on communications speed. The technology already exists, the manufacturers just have to talk to each other.

Inexpensive business phone systems will provide home offices with the same capabilities as giant corporations

AT&T's System 2000 phone system already offers most of the sophisticated features of units costing several times more money. Every home office already has powerful FAX systems.

Tax incentives will be offered companies that allow people to work from their home as well as to home-based businesses

This one is harder to predict as it involves overcoming the powerful lobbyists of large corporations. As air pollution, traffic jams and limited office space make their impact felt, it will happen.

Computer hardware and software will get cheaper

Even now, Intel is beginning to discuss details of the 80586 chip, even before most software can really take advantage of the 80386 chip!

People will become comfortable with computers

We are now raising a generation of computer literates. Whether it is through good schools or video games, the average teenager feels comfortable with computers in a way his parents never could. The level of general technical competence will rise. Less time will have to be spent teaching users how to do simple tasks.

Programs will learn to talk to each other

Currently both the MAC and the PC fail at allowing programs to communicate with each other and allowing data changed in one program to be reflected in another.

Home offices will be respected

It is still common for home workers to find that banks, credit card companies and even friends do not readily accept their lifestyle. This will change as more people work from home. This will constitute the single largest change in the lives of home workers.

This is a glimpse of what technology holds for home offices in the future. 26 million people now work from their homes and the trend is accelerating even as you read. Actual electronic resources available to home computers will grow even faster than it has in the past for this reason alone. With more and more home workers the larger market will attract more and more companies looking to earn money by providing what we need.

If you have already launched your home office, congratulations. You are riding the crest of the new economic wave of the future. If you have not, what are you waiting for? All of us have heard those sad "if only if" stories of people who let opportunities slip through their fingers like grains of sand. This is your opportunity. Ride the wave, don't let your future success be washed away.